DON JUAN

NOTES

including

- *Life and Background*
- *Stanza, Style, and Plan*
- *List of Characters*
- *Synopsis*
- *Summaries and Commentaries*
- *Notes on Main Characters*
- *Review Questions and Essay Topics*
- *Selected Bibliography*

by
Dougald B. MacEachen, Ph.D.
Department of English
John Carroll University

INCORPORATED

LINCOLN, NEBRASKA 68501

Editor

Gary Carey, M.A.
University of Colorado

Consulting Editor

James L. Roberts, Ph.D.
Department of English
University of Nebraska

ISBN 0-8220-0411-9
© Copyright 1970
by
C. K. Hillegass
All Rights Reserved
Printed in U.S.A.

1991 Printing

Cliffs Notes, Inc.   Lincoln, Nebraska

CONTENTS

Introduction 5

Life of Byron 6

The Literary Background 8

The "Ottava Rima" Stanza and Style 9

Plan of the Poem 11

Style of the Poem 11

List of Characters 12

A Brief Synopsis 16

Summaries and Critical Commentaries 23

Notes on Main Characters

    Don Juan 77
    Donna Julia 78
    Haidée 78
    Lambro 79
    John Johnson 79
    Gulbeyaz 80
    Suwarrow 80
    Catherine the Great 81
    Lord Henry Amundeville 81
    Lady Adeline Amundeville 82
    Aurora Raby 83

Review Questions and Theme Topics 83

Selected Bibliography 86

Don Juan Notes

INTRODUCTION

Like Chaucer's *Canterbury Tales,* Byron's *Don Juan* is an unfinished poem. How Byron might have ended it is idle speculation. It could have gone on indefinitely like a comic strip as long as the public showed an interest in its continuation. All Byron had to do was to change the locale and introduce new episodes. Byron spoke once or twice of letting Juan be killed off in the French Revolution. That would have made a suitable conclusion to a drifting, planless life just as the Greek revolution made a suitable, even immortalizing, conclusion to Byron's drifting, planless life. He could have had Empress Catherine, or her son Paul I, transfer her envoy to France, perhaps as a spy, and have him blunder into the guillotine while being pursued by some beautiful goddess of reason. Such an ending would have been consistent with the personality and character of Juan, who is swept along with the current, who does not seek out but is sought out.

Don Juan is such a vast creation that it is difficult to judge it as a whole. It has something for every kind of reader and a good deal that will please no reader. There are numerous dull stanzas in it in which Byron says or does nothing of interest. To borrow a word used by Byron near the beginning of the poem, it has its *longueurs,* or tedious passages. Byron's skepticism and cynicism become tiresome. His hero, Don Juan, as sometimes happens in novels, is of less interest than several of his other characters, even though he does develop and is more mature in Canto XVI than in Canto I. But he never develops a strong moral sense. In regard to sex he remains amoral, or so it would seem. He remains a drifter, although he becomes a better judge of human nature as the poem progresses.

But granting some weaknesses in structure, characterization, and philosophy of life, *Don Juan* is an epic carnival, as Truman

Guy Steffan calls it in his *The Making of a Masterpiece*. It has scope, variety of human types and experience, common sense, much matter for laughter, clever and witty observation, ease, and fluency. It may not reveal a wealth of learning and a depth of thought and insight, but it does reveal a wide range of experience derived from books and from life. An index of the topics in *Don Juan* would be very long. In some parts it is unsurpassed by anything of a similar kind in English poetry before it, for instance, the Don Juan — Donna Julia episode, the development of the love affair between Don Juan and Haidée, and the savage, mocking indictment of war. Last, it gives us a great deal of Byron himself, one of the most interesting personalities of English literature.

LIFE OF BYRON

George Noel Gordon, Lord Byron, was born in London on January 22, 1788, the only son of Captain John Byron and his second wife, the heiress Catherine Gordon. On the insistence of the Gordon family, John Byron legally changed his name to John Gordon. As a result, Lord Byron was born a Gordon and not a Byron. On the death of his granduncle, William, Lord Byron, the poet inherited the family title and estate.

Byron attended a number of schools, including the famous public school, Harrow, where he made many friends. From Harrow he went to Trinity College, Cambridge. He received an M.A. degree from Cambridge in 1808.

Byron's first volume of poems, *Fugitive Pieces,* was privately printed in 1806. A selection of poems from *Fugitive Pieces* and other juvenilia were published as *Poems on Various Occasions. Poems* was republished as *Hours of Idleness* the following year, with Byron's name on the title page. *Hours of Idleness* was unfavorably reviewed by the influential *Edinburgh Review* in 1807. Byron never forgot the reception given to his first acknowledged volume of poetry and in 1809 anonymously took revenge on the anonymous *Edinburgh* reviewer in *English*

Bards and Scotch Reviewers, in which he showed himself to be an able satirist in the manner of Pope, of whom he was always a strong admirer.

In July, 1809, Byron set out on his "grand tour," which included Portugal, Spain, Albania, Greece, and Turkey. His impressions of these countries formed the substance of *Childe Harold's Pilgrimage,* Cantos I and II, published in 1812. *Childe Harold* became immensely popular and Byron was lionized by London high society. The success of *Childe Harold* encouraged Byron to write a series of tales with a Turkish or Greek background, all of which sold well.

Early in 1815 Byron married Anne Isabella Milbanke. A year later his wife left him, taking with her their daughter, Augusta Ada Byron. A separation was later arranged. The society which had made Byron famous blamed him for the separation and ostracized him. In 1816 Byron left England, never to return.

Canto III of *Childe Harold* and "The Prisoner of Chillon" appeared in the fall of 1816. These two works are among Byron's best non-satirical poetry. In them Byron showed a verbal felicity and a command of metaphor not to be found in his earlier poetry. In 1818 Byron published *Childe Harold,* Canto IV, inferior in interest to *Childe Harold,* Canto III, because it was overloaded with archeological materials suggested by a trip Byron made from Venice to Rome.

"Beppo," published also in 1818, marks the appearance of the new poetic manner on which Byron's present reputation as a poet largely rests. "Beppo," in *ottava rima,* introduces Byron the humorist to the poetry-reading public. Shortly after the appearance of "Beppo," Byron began his great masterpiece, *Don Juan.*

In 1821 and 1822 Byron made a bid for fame in the field of drama. In fifteen months he wrote four five-act plays, *Sardanapalus, Marino Falieri, The Two Foscari,* and *Werner.* These are generally considered Byron's least readable poetry. During the same period he wrote *Cain,* a play in three acts, and two dramatic fragments, *Heaven and Earth* and *The Deformed Transformed.*

In 1822 one of Byron's most perfect poems, and one of the best satires in English poetry, "The Vision of Judgment," was published in John Hunt's periodical, *The Liberal*. "The Vision of Judgment," in *ottava rima*, is an amusing attack on George III, George IV, and on the poet laureate, Robert Southey.

Byron returned to *Don Juan* in 1822 and by May, 1823, had written a total of sixteen cantos. The poem was published in six separate volumes between 1819 and 1823.

Byron had lived in various parts of Italy from his arrival in that country in 1816. In July, 1823, he left Italy for Greece to help the Greeks in their struggle to free themselves from Turkish rule. He died of a fever at Missolonghi, Greece, on April 19, 1823.

THE LITERARY BACKGROUND

The character of Don Juan was contributed to world literature by the Spanish writer Gabriel Tellez (1584-1648), whose pen name was Tirso de Molina, in his play *El Burlador de Sevilla (The Rogue of Seville)*, which appeared in the early 1630s. The character of the unscrupulous seducer became a favorite with later writers, and of all literary characters Don Juan is the one who is most used, in plays, in pantomimes, and in narrative verse. Mozart's *Don Giovanni* is an example of the use of the Don Juan character in opera. Few other literary characters approach Don Juan in popularity. Readers and lovers of the theater seem to be fascinated by the theme of the "lady-killer." The bibliography of the Don Juan theme fills a whole volume.

How Byron became acquainted with the Don Juan legend is not known, but it would have been impossible for a well-read poet like Byron not to have become acquainted with it. In the first stanza of Canto I he writes:

> I want a hero. . . .
> I'll therefore take our ancient friend Don Juan —
> We all have seen him, in the pantomime,
> Sent to the Devil somewhat ere his time.

In Byron's day a pantomime based on the Restoration dramatist Thomas Shadwell's Don Juan play, *The Libertine,* was frequently presented on the London stage. He could also have become acquainted with the legend through Shadwell's play or through Molière's Don Juan play, *The Banquet of Stone,* or through Carlo Goldoni's play, *Don Juan Tenorio,* or through Mozart. Don Juan was a familiar public figure in the early nineteenth century.

The idea of using Don Juan as a centralizing character in an episodic poem may have been suggested to Byron by his immensely successful *Childe Harold's Pilgrimage,* a discursive, descriptive and reflective poem that is held together by the character of Childe Harold. Byron himself was a Don Juan character and so was his spendthrift father, John Byron.

How Byron became acquainted with the *Don Juan* manner and form we know from his letters. A minor contemporary poet, John Hookham Frere, using the pseudonym Whistlecraft had written a poem which appeared in 1817 with the title "Prospectus and Specimen of an Intended National Work, by William and Robert Whistlecraft, of Stowmarket, in Suffolk, Harness and Collar Makers, Intended to Comprise the Most Interesting Particulars Relating to King Arthur and His Round Table." The poem was expanded and appeared in 1818 with the title "The Monks and the Giants." Byron was delighted with the mixture of the serious and the comic in the poem and resolved to write a digressive poem in a similar manner. The result was "Beppo." The public and Byron's friends were pleased with "Beppo," and as a result Byron decided to write a long poem using the style and the stanza he had used in "Beppo." The poem was *Don Juan.*

THE *OTTAVA RIMA* STANZA AND STYLE

Behind the character of Don Juan lay a long tradition going back to the Renaissance. Behind the stanza used in "Prospectus" and "Beppo" also lay a long tradition going back to the

Renaissance. These two traditions are combined in *Don Juan*. Chief among the Italian Renaissance writers who had combined serious and comic matter are Luigi Pulci (1432-84) and Francesco Berni (1496?-1535). The tradition was carried on in the eighteenth century by Giambattista Casti. After becoming acquainted with the mock-heroic manner in Frere, Byron steeped himself in its Italian practitioners. He had begun to study Italian in 1810, and was particularly fond of Casti.

Ottava rima, or eight-line stanza, was the poetic form favored by the Italian satirical writers of mock-heroic romances. The rhyme scheme of *ottava rima,* abababcc, is a demanding one and for that very reason encouraged the use of comic rhyme such as Byron employed so extensively in *Don Juan.* The concluding couplet can be used to end the stanza with a witticism or a swift fall from the lofty to the low or a surprise for the reader in the form of a pair of unexpected and clever comic rhymes. Byron, as a devoted disciple of Pope, who wrote almost exclusively in iambic pentameter couplets, was fond of couplets and for this reason alone would have found the *ottava rima* stanza attractive. In the course of writing *Don Juan* Byron became very skilled in the handling of the challenging rhyme scheme of *ottava rima.* His ability to create outrageous rhyme is unrivaled. His mastery of his stanza pattern pleases the reader, whether he is aware of it or not. *Ottava rima* helped to make Byron the great comic writer that he is.

For example, in the first stanza of Canto XIII Byron writes:

> I now mean to be serious; — it is time,
>> Since Laughter now-a-days is deemed too serious;
> A jest at Vice by Virtue's called a crime,
>> And critically held as deleterious:
> Besides, the sad's a source of the sublime,
>> Although, when long, a little apt to weary us;
> And therefore shall my lay soar high and solemn,
> As an old temple dwindled to a column.

In this stanza Byron alternates masculine (single) with feminine (double) rhymes and concludes with feminine rhymes. The rhymes are perfect and pleasing to the ear. In addition, in his climactic concluding line he coins a simile that is both fresh and striking. Italy, where Byron wrote his *Don Juan,* is full of "old temples dwindled to a column."

PLAN OF THE POEM

Byron made contradictory statements about his purpose in writing *Don Juan.* He told his friend Thomas Moore in 1818 that the poem was meant "to be a little quietly facetious upon every thing," and to his publisher John Murray he wrote that in *Don Juan* he intended only "to giggle and to make giggle" and had no other plan for the poem. Later, in 1820, he wrote Moore: *"Don Juan* will be known by and bye, for what it is intended, — a Satire on *abuses* of the present states of Society. . . ." His purpose in writing *Don Juan* can best be deduced from a reading of the poem. It is both quietly facetious on everything and a serious satire on the hypocrisies of high society, the false glory associated with war, man's pursuit of fame, the little devices by which people try to deceive themselves, the human penchant for rationalization, and much else. In *Don Juan* Byron shows himself to be a humorist in the great tradition; he belongs in the company of Chaucer, Shakespeare, Ben Jonson, William Congreve, Richard Sheridan, Henry Fielding, Laurence Sterne, and his contemporary Jane Austen.

STYLE OF THE POEM

In general, the style of *Don Juan* is the easy conversational or epistolary style. Byron is talking to his readers and as he talks his subject reminds him of this or that, to which a few lines or stanzas will thereupon be devoted. *Don Juan* is deliberately discursive and digressive.

Byron does not always use a conversational tone. In the stanzas on the religious feelings which twilight can arouse in him (Canto III, Sts. 102-08) Byron writes in the inflated Romantic manner. When writing about Tom's thwarted attempt to rob Don Juan, he descends to slang (Canto XI, Sts. 10-19).

LIST OF CHARACTERS IN *DON JUAN*
(In Order of Appearance)

Don Juan

The son of an easygoing father and a strict mother who is doted on by his parents. At the age of sixteen he has an affair with Donna Julia.

Don José

Juan's father, who is unfaithful to his wife and careless of his reputation.

Donna Inez

Juan's mother, a learned woman plagued by the infidelity of her husband. One of her chief interests is the education of her son.

The Narrator

A friend of Don Juan's family. He is dismissed from the story in the first canto and his place is taken by the omniscient author.

Donna Julia

The wife of Don Alfonso and a friend of Don Juan's family. She is twenty-three and unhappily married.

Don Alfonso

The husband of Donna Julia. He is fifty and fails to provide his wife with the love she yearns for.

Antonia

Donna Julia's maidservant who helps her in her intrigue with Don Juan.

Pedrillo

Juan's tutor, the victim of cannibalism by the survivors of the wreck of the *Trinidada*.

Haidée

The beautiful seventeen-year-old daughter of Lambro, a Greek smuggler, pirate, and slave trader, and of a Moroccan mother who has died before the story opens.

Lambro

A sternly inflexible and completely self-controlled man who, because his native country is not free, preys upon the commerce of all countries. Haidée is his most treasured possession.

Zoe

Haidée's faithful maidservant and companion. She is "wiser than Haidée by a year or two."

Raucocanti

A member of an Italian operatic troupe sold into slavery by their treacherous manager. On the slave ship carrying them to Constantinople, he entertains Juan with malicious character sketches of the other members of the troupe.

John Johnson

A cynical but practical English soldier of fortune captured by the Turks while fighting with the Russians. Like Juan, he is sold as a slave.

Baba

A eunuch in the harem of the Sultan of Turkey who is the trusted servant of the sultana. He is shrewd and reliable.

Gulbeyaz

The twenty-six-year-old fourth (and favorite) wife of the Turkish sultan. She has seen the handsome Juan on his way to the slave market and sends Baba to buy him.

The Sultan

The ruler of the Turkish Empire who has four wives and 1,500 concubines. He is fifty-nine, solemn, cruel, unscrupulous, lazy, and ignorant. He has fifty daughters and forty-eight sons.

The Mother of the Maids

The woman who is responsible for maintaining discipline in the sultan's harem.

Lolah

A dusky beauty who is a concubine in the sultan's harem.

Katinka

A harem beauty from Russian Georgia. Both she and Lolah volunteer to share their beds with "Juanna."

Dudù

A "kind of sleepy Venus," a "large, and languishing, and lazy" beauty. Since there is no bed in the harem for Juan (dressed as a girl by Baba), Dudù has to share her bed with "Juanna."

Suwarrow

Byron's name for General Suvorov (or Suvaroff), a historical character, one of the ablest generals in the armies of Catherine the Great. He is in charge of the Russian forces that capture Ismail from the Turks.

Leila

A ten-year-old Turkish orphan whose parents have been killed during the assault on the Turkish fortress of Ismail.

Catherine the Great

The sixty-one-year-old Czarina of Russia who falls in love with Don Juan.

Tom

The English robber who in a holdup attempt on Don Juan is mortally wounded by him.

Lady Pinchbeck

The woman selected by Don Juan to supervise the upbringing of his orphan ward Leila.

Lord Henry Amundeville

A wealthy young English nobleman who is a member of the Privy Council and who becomes a friend of Don Juan.

Lady Adeline Amundeville

The socially efficient twenty-one-year-old wife of Lord Henry who decides that she must get Don Juan married to save him from designing females like the Duchess Fitz-Fulke.

The Duchess Fitz-Fulke

A voluptuous, intriguing, fun-loving friend of the Amunde-villes. She and her husband get along by never spending any time together.

Aurora Raby

A sixteen-year-old orphan heiress and friend of the Amunde-villes. She is the only Roman Catholic in her social circle. She is pious, austere, sincere, and charitable. Like other young ladies, she becomes interested in the handsome Don Juan. She is the last character introduced into *Don Juan*.

SYNOPSIS

CANTO I

Don Juan was born in Seville, Spain, the son of Don José, a member of the nobility, and Donna Inez, a woman of considerable learning. Juan's parents did not get along well with each other because Don José was interested in women rather than in knowledge and was unfaithful to Donna Inez. Donna Inez was on the point of suing her husband for divorce when he died of a fever. The education of Juan became the primary interest of his mother. She saw to it that he received a thorough training in the arts and sciences but took great care that he should learn nothing about the basic facts of life.

Among Donna Inez's friends is Donna Julia, the young and beautiful wife of Don Alfonso, a middle-aged man incapable of engaging her affections. When Juan is sixteen, Donna Julia falls in love with the handsome young man and finds opportunities to be in his company. One midsummer evening the two declare their love for each other. In November of that year Don Alfonso comes one night to the bedroom of his wife accompanied by a crowd of his friends. When he enters the room, his wife and her maid are ready for him; the bedclothes have been piled up in a heap on the bed. Don Alfonso and his followers search Donna Julia's suite for a lover but find none. While searching, Don Alfonso becomes the target of a tirade of abuse from his wife. The whole company leaves, crestfallen. Don Alfsonso soon returns to apologize and happens to find a pair of men's shoes in his wife's bedroom. He leaves the room to get his sword. Don Juan, who has been hidden under the heap of bedclothes, prepares to make his escape by a back exit and runs into Don Alfsonso. In the fight that ensues, Juan strikes Alfonso on the nose and makes his escape.

The sequel to these events is that Donna Julia is sent to a convent and Don Alfonso sues for divorce. Donna Inez decides that her son should spend the next four years traveling.

CANTO II

Don Juan embarks on a ship bound for Leghorn, Italy, where his family has relatives. Not long after the ship leaves port, a violent storm drives it off its course. In spite of everything the crew can do, the ship finally goes down with most of its passengers. Only as many as can fit in a small cutter and a long-boat are saved. Then the cutter is swamped and the nine men in it drown. The men in the longboat, including Juan and his tutor, are reduced to eating shoe leather. At this point one of the survivors suggests cannibalism as a means of survival. The lot falls on Juan's tutor. The arrival of the boat at an island prevents the sacrifice of a second victim. The boat is driven against a reef and overturns. By this time only Juan and three others are left alive. By clinging to an oar Juan is swept to the shore and manages to crawl up on the beach, where he promptly collapses. The three others perish.

CANTO III

When Juan at last opens his eyes, he sees a lovely young face peering into his. It is Haidée, the only daughter of a Greek freebooter who has made the isolated Aegean island his head-quarters. Haidée and her maid help the weak and emaciated Juan to a cave, where they gradually nurse him back to health. Haidée does not dare bring Juan into her home, for she knows that her father would sell him as a slave. Inevitably Juan and Haidée fall in love and marry without benefit of clergy. A month after Juan's arrival, Lambro, Haidée's father, takes his fleet on a piratical expedition. Some time later word is brought back that Lambro has died. Juan and Haidée move into his mansion as man and wife. But the rumor of Lambro's death is false. When he returns to his island port and walks toward his house, he is surprised to see people idling, feasting, and entertaining themselves. He does not make his presence known immediately. At the time of his arrival, Juan and Haidée, attired in gorgeous costumes, are feasting in Lambro's dining hall and being entertained by a minstrel.

CANTO IV

After dining, Juan and Haidée take their siesta. Haidée, for the first time, has an ominous nightmare. She dreams that she is in a cave and that Juan lies at her feet, wet and cold and lifeless. While she is gazing on his face, his features slowly change into those of her stern father. She awakes and there before her stands the supposedly dead Lambro. When she arises and shrieks, she awakes Juan. Clinging to him, she tells him that the intruder is her father and beseeches him to beg his forgiveness. She pleads with her father to spare Juan. Lambro quietly commands Juan to surrender the saber he has snatched from the wall. When Juan refuses, Haidée's father draws and cocks his pistol. Haidée saves Juan's life by throwing herself in front of him. Her father replaces his pistol in its holster and blows a whistle. At once twenty of his followers appear and attack Juan, who succeeds in wounding two of them before being twice wounded himself. When Haidée sees Juan cut down, a vein bursts in her body and she collapses. For days she lies in a coma. When she finally regains consciousness, she is apathetic and speechless. The singing of a harpist at last draws from her the response of tears. Then she arises and

lies at all those around her as if they were foes. Soon she lapses
nto apathy again, and after twelve days she dies. Juan has been
:arried on board one of Lambro's ships, where he finds himself
n the company of several other captives. Not long after, he is
>rought to a slave market in Constantinople.

CANTO V

In the slave market Juan and a fellow captive, an English-
nan named Johnson, are bought by the eunuch Baba for Gul-
>eyaz, the fourth wife of the sultan, who has seen Juan being led
o the market and who wants him for herself. They are brought
o the royal palace, where Juan is dressed in woman's clothes.
'Juanna" is then conducted to the sultana's apartment. She com-
nands him to make love to her. But he is still faithful to the
nemory of Haidée and burst into tears. The sultana throws her
.rms around him, but Juan disengages himself. At first, the
ultana is enraged, but her mood soon changes to tears. Her
:ears move Juan and he "began to stammer some excuses," but
.t this point the interview is ended by the announcement that
he sultan is coming. The sultan notices Juan among the sultana's
vomen and remarks that it is a pity that a Christian should be so
>retty. This remark draws the glances of all to the person of Juan.

CANTO VI

Juan is placed in an apartment of the palace where many of
he sultan's concubines are quartered, for it is assumed that he is
. new member of the sultan's large harem. He is assigned to a
>retty girl named Dudù as a companion. During the night the
vhole harem is awakened by a loud scream from Dudù. She is
>ressed for an explanation. She has dreamed, she says, that she
vas walking in a wood in which there was a tree with a golden
.pple. The golden apple fell at her feet, but when she picked it
.p to bite into it, a bee flew out and stung her. The eunuch Baba
eports the next morning to the sultana that Juan and Dudù shared
[uarters during the night but says nothing of the dream. When

Gulbeyaz hears this, her cheeks become ashen. She commands Baba to bring Juan and Dudù to her.

CANTO VII

The setting of Canto VII is Ismail, a Turkish fortress on the Danube, which is being besieged by the Russians. Here arrive by steps which Byron omits, a party from Constantinople made up of Juan, Johnson, two unidentified Turkish women, and a eunuch. They are brought to General Suwarrow, the ruthless and efficient commander of the Russians. Johnson had served in the Russian army before, and Suwarrow assigns him to his old regiment. Juan he assigns to himself. Johnson requests the general that the Turkish ladies and their attendant be given kind treatment because they have helped himself and Juan escape from Constantinople.

CANTO VIII

The final assault on Ismail begins. The Turks resist with valor and before the fortress is captured rivers of blood have been shed. Juan, swept away by a thirst for glory, proves himself to be a soldier of prowess and courage, but at the same time shows his humanitarianism by rescuing a little Turkish orphan girl from a pair of Cossacks who are about to slay her. Juan, now a lieutenant in the Russian army, is selected because of his valor and humanity to carry the news of the victory to the Empress Catherine in Petersburgh. He takes Leila, the young Turkish girl, with him.

CANTO IX

The Empress Catherine is so much taken with the appearance of the handsome youthful lieutenant that when he presents her with his dispatch, she does not at once break the seal. When she finally does so, she is filled with joy. She falls in love at first sight with the bearer of the good news. Juan is swept off his feet by the attention he receives from Catherine. She promptly makes him a favorite and showers him with wealth. Because of the position he so quickly gains and because of his gracious demeanor, he becomes the center of attention in the Russian court.

CANTO X

Juan soon finds himself quite at home in Petersburgh and "Seduced by Youth and dangerous examples" grows a little dissipated. He lives "in a hurry/ Of waste and haste, and glare, and gloss and glitter." He is courted by everyone. For a while all goes well; then he falls sick. The doctors conclude that the climate is too cold for him, and Catherine, much against her wishes, decides to send him on an official mission to England. He leaves Russia for England laden with gifts and honors, taking with him his little orphan Leila.

CANTO XI

In England Juan quickly becomes the object of as much attention as he had been in Russia. He is known to have come on an important mission; he is handsome, young, and accomplished; he knows several languages; and "Some rumour also of some strange adventures/ Had gone before him, and his wars and loves." He is well received everywhere. He passes his mornings in business, his afternoons in visits, and his evenings in dancing and other forms of entertainment.

CANTO XII

One of Juan's first problems to be solved in England is what to do with little Leila. He finally decides to place her in the care of Lady Pinchbeck, who is elderly, virtuous, wise in the ways of the world, and interested in the Turkish orphan.

CANTO XIII-XIV

Diplomatic business often brings Juan in contact with Lord Henry Amundeville, who takes a liking to the young Spaniard, as does his wife, Lady Adeline. Juan is frequently a guest in Lord Henry's mansion in London. When the winter season in London is over, the Amundevilles leave for their country estate, Norman Abbey.

When autumn comes the Amundevilles invite a large number of guests, including Juan, to the abbey. Juan acquits himself well in the country. He proves to be good at fox-hunting, riding, dancing, and all the other activities of country life among the aristocracy. Lady Fitz-Fulke, who is living apart from her husband, begins to take a special interest in him. When Lady Adeline notices this, she resolves to save Juan from Lady Fitz-Fulke, who has a reputation for getting involved in intrigues. Lady Adeline has a weakness of her own: her heart is vacant. She loves her husband, or thinks she does, but that love costs her an effort. She is also of the same age as Juan, namely twenty-one.

CANTO XV

Lady Adeline tells Juan that she thinks he ought to get married. Juan makes a polite reply. She names a number of what she considers good matches but fails to mention Aurora Raby, who is rich, noble, young, pretty, sincere, and a Catholic like Juan. This omission makes Juan wonder and he brings the fact to the attention of Adeline. Lady Adeline marvels " 'what he saw in such a baby/ As that prim, silent, cold Aurora Raby?' " (Canto XV, St. 49) One evening Juan sits beside Aurora at dinner. She pays no attention to him, a phenomenon which piques him and arouses his interest in her.

CANTO XVI

That night Juan, unable to sleep, walks out into a gallery filled with portraits of the eminent or beautiful dead. Much to his astonishment he sees a monk in cowl, robe, and beads. The monk slowly walks by him and disappears. As Juan has heard that the ghost of a monk haunts Norman Abbey, in his fear he assumes that he has seen this very ghost.

The next morning Juan is unusually pensive at breakfast. Lord Henry remarks that he looks as if he had seen the ghost of the Black Friar. Juan does not admit what he has seen. Adeline then sings the song of the Black Friar, a song she has composed about the ghost of Norman Abbey. The song restores Juan's spirits.

That night Juan is again unable to sleep and again he hears the deliberate footsteps he heard the night before. Suddenly his door flies open. In the doorway stands the friar. Juan's dread turns to anger and he advances toward the ghost. The ghost retreats until it is backed up against a wall. Juan stretches out his arm and touches the solid breast of "her frolic Grace — Fitz-Fulke!"

CANTO XVII
(A Fragment of Fourteen Stanzas)

The following morning Juan looks "wan and worn." The Duchess Fitz-Fulke "had a sort of air rebuked—/ Seemed pale and shivered. . ." (St. 14).

SUMMARIES AND COMMENTARIES

DEDICATION

Summary

Robert Southey and William Wordsworth, who have both sold themselves to the king, would like to be considered the greatest poets of the age. Posterity will decide whether they or Walter Scott, Samuel Rogers, Thomas Campbell, Thomas Moore, and George Crabbe will enjoy the largest share of fame. As for Byron, he is not competing with them, for he does not consider himself a poet in the sense that they are. His muse is a pedestrian one.

Would Milton, if he were alive, obey the "intellectual eunuch" Castlereagh, as Southey and Wordsworth do? Castlereagh is a tongue-tied oppressor, a tool of tyranny, and a bungler.

The poet dedicates *Don Juan* to Robert Southey, who sings the praises of tyrants and who is an apostate from political liberalism.

Commentary

The Dedication, written in 1818, was withheld from publication, on the insistence of John Murray, Byron's publisher, until after Byron's death. Byron kept up a running quarrel with the poet laureate, Robert Southey, for years, for poetical, political, and personal reasons, and finally demolished him in his superb "The Vision of Judgment."

The savage attack on Robert Stewart, Viscount Castlereagh, Foreign Secretary in the reactionary Tory government from 1812 to his suicide in 1822, was motivated by Byron's political liberalism, which tended to be extremist. Castlereagh, an able cabinet minister who did much to make possible Wellington's victory over Napolen and to save England from defeat, was an unselfish patriot but no sympathizer with self-rule or democracy.

CANTO I

Summary

The author begins by saying that since his own age cannot supply a suitable hero for his poem, he will use an old friend, Don Juan. Don Juan was born in Seville, Spain. His parents are Don José and Donna Inez. Donna Inez is learned and has a good memory. Her favorite science is mathematics. She has a smattering of Greek, Latin, French, English, and Hebrew. Don José has no love for learning or the learned and has a roving eye. As his wife is rigidly virtuous and as he is incautious by nature, he is forever getting into scrapes. Consequently, there are quarrels between the two. Donna Inez, with the help of druggists and doctors, tries to prove that her husband is mad. She also keeps a diary in which she notes all his faults and even searches through his trunks of books and letters looking for evidence to use against him. Their friends and relatives try to no avail to bring about a reconciliation; their lawyers recommend a divorce. But before the situation can reach a critical point, Don José dies.

Donna Inez makes herself responsible for the supervision of Don Juan's education. He is taught riding, fencing, gunnery, how to scale a fortress, languages, sciences, and arts. His education is to a certain degree impractical, for he is taught nothing about life and studies the classics from expurgated editions. In short, his mother sees to it that he receives an education calculated to repress all his natural instincts and keeps the facts of life from him.

Among Donna Inez's friends is Donna Julia, a beautiful, intelligent young woman with Moorish blood in her veins. She is married to Don Alfonso, a jealous man more than twice her age. Theirs is a loveless marriage. It is rumored that Donna Inez and Don Alfonso had once been lovers and that she cultivated the friendship of Donna Julia to maintain the association with the husband. Donna Julia has always been fond of Juan, but when he becomes a young man of sixteen, her feelings toward him change and become a source of embarrassment to both of them. Juan does not understand the change that is taking place in him, but the more sophisticated Julia realizes that she is falling in love with Juan. She resolves to fight her growing love and never to see Juan again but the next day finds a reason for visiting his mother. She then convinces herself that her love is only Platonic and persuades herself that it will remain that way. Juan meantime cannot understand why he is pensive and inclined to seek solitude.

One June evening Julia and Juan happen to be in a bower together. One of Julia's hands happens to fall on one of Juan's. When the sun sets and the moon rises, Juan's arm finds its way around Julia's waist. Julia strives with herself a little, "And whispering 'I will ne'er consent'—consented" (St. 117).

As Julia lies in her bed one November night, there arises a tremendous clatter. Her maid Antonia warns her that Don Alfonso is coming up the stairs with half the city at his back. The two women have barely enough time to throw the bedclothes in a heap when Don Alfonso enters the room. Julia indignantly asks Alfonso if he suspects her of wrongdoing and invites him to search the room. Alfonso and his followers do so and find nothing. While the search is going on, Donna Julia protests her innocence with angry eloquence, giving numerous examples of her virtue and pouring abuse upon her luckless husband. When no lover is found, Don Alfonso tries to excuse his behavior but only succeeds in drawing sobs and hysterics from his wife. Alfonso, shamefaced, withdraws with his followers and Julia and Antonia bolt the bedroom door.

No sooner has Alfonso gone than Juan emerges from beneath the pile of bedclothes where he has been hidden. Knowing that Alfonso would soon be back, Julia and Antonia advise Juan to go into a closet. Hardly has Juan entered his new hiding place when Alfonso returns. Alfonso makes various excuses for his conduct and begs Julia's pardon, which she half gives and half withholds. The matter might have ended there had Alfonso not stumbled over a pair of men's shoes. He promptly goes to get his sword. Julia immediately urges Juan to leave the room and make his exit by the garden gate, the key to which she gives him. Unfortunately, on his way out he meets Alfonso and knocks him down. In the scuffle Juan loses his only garment and flees naked into the night.

Alfonso sues for divorce. Juan's mother decides that her son should leave Seville and travel to various European countries for four years. Julia is put in a convent from which she sends Juan a letter confessing her love for him and expressing no regrets.

The first episode of *Don Juan* ends at this point, but before concluding Canto I Byron adds twenty-two stanzas in which he entertains himself by giving a mocking statement of his intentions in regard to *Don Juan*, taunts his contemporaries Wordsworth, Coleridge, and Southey, defends the morality of his story, confesses that at thirty his hair is gray and his heart has lost its freshness, comments on the evanescence of fame, and says goodbye to his readers.

Commentary

In the first few stanzas, Byron establishes the half-playful and mocking and half-serious tone that is going to pervade *Don Juan*. When that is done, he gives his readers as the chief characters in his first canto a pair of married couples. They are both unhappily married. Don José and Donna Inez are mismated. Donna Inez is a cold and severe type of woman, although she has evidently not always been so. It was generally known that in her younger days she had had an affair with Don Alfonso. Don José is a good-natured, easy-going kind of man inclined to take his pleasures where he finds them. Byron's defense of him is that he had been badly brought up and that he was amorous by nature. In the character of Donna Inez, Byron was satirizing, against the advice of his friends, his estranged wife, Lady Byron. Donna Julia and Don Alfonso are mismated by age as Donna Inez and Don José are mismated by incompatibility of character and personality. Don Alfonso has nothing to offer Donna Julia except his name and station. Theirs was a marriage of convenience. Byron does not bother to devote much characterization to Don Alfonso. He merely says he was neither very lovable nor very hatable. He had a more or less negative personality, neither warm nor cold. Like any other husband, he did not care to be cuckolded.

Byron is far more interested in the wives than in the husbands and characterizes them rather extensively. Neither portrait is flattering. Donna Inez's is clearly malicious; in her Byron was attacking his estranged wife. She is not a faithless wife, but she is an intolerant and rather frigid one. Donna Julia's portrait of woman as wife is likewise unflattering; she deceives herself—and her husband. However, Byron makes the reader feel sympathetic toward her in spite of his using her to show up woman's wiles. Donna Julia and Don José, had they been closer in age, might have made a compatible pair; Donna Julia finds in Don José's son the warmth that was in the father. Donna Inez and Don Alfonso, who had been lovers at one time, might have gotten along well in marriage. Human nature and society, Byron seems to say, work against a happy marriage.

Some of Byron's contemporaries found Byron's bedroom farce immoral. It can be said in his defense that his mocking presentation neutralizes any remote occasion of sin that there might be present in his story of illicit love. Nor does he supply any provocative details. Lastly, both Donna Julia and Don Juan are made to look ridiculous, and both are punished for their guilt.

The story in Canto I is told by an "I" *persona* who is said to be a friend of Don Juan's family. Byron may have foreseen the difficulties involved in making this *persona* a witness who would be present with Don Juan in his various adventures and so decided to discard him. At any rate the "I" narrator is discarded before the first canto ends, and becomes Byron himself giving his opinions on various matters and communicating more or less confidentially with the reader.

Canto I of *Don Juan* is without doubt the most interesting, entertaining, and amusing of all the cantos. For anything of this kind comparable in quality and liveliness in English verse, the reader has to go all the way back to Chaucer.

CANTO II

Summary

At Cadiz, Spain, Juan boards the ship *Trinidada* bound for Leghorn, Italy, where he is to visit relatives settled there. His suite consists of three servants and a tutor. As Juan has no experience on shipboard, he promptly becomes seasick. Hardly has the ship set sail when a storm blows up. Even though the crew takes in sail, the rough seas tear away the *Trinidada's* rudder, and the pumps have to be manned, for the ship has sprung a leak. The men try in vain to plug the leak by stuffing cloth into it. A sudden squall lays the ship over on its beam ends. The crew immediately cut away the masts and the ship rights itself. In desperation the men try to get at the liquor supply, but Juan shows his intrepidity by holding them off with a pair of pistols.

Without a rudder, masts, or sails, and leaking so badly that the pumps are useless, the ship lies rolling helplessly in the trough of the waves and at length begins settling by the head. Some of the crew manage to get the cutter and the longboat off the ship and to salvage a little food and drinking water. The other boats have been stove in during the storm. Anything that would support a man is thrown overboard. The two boats have hardly been lowered, when the ship sinks, carrying with it almost two hundred men. Only thirty-nine, Don Juan and his tutor among them, manage to save their lives. Soon the number is reduced to thirty, for the little cutter with nine men aboard is swamped by the towering waves. The men in the longboat manage to keep it afloat and even rig up a sail and mast out of two blankets and an oar. At length there comes a calm, and the bone-weary men get some sleep for the first time in three days. When they awake they are ravenous and promptly devour all of their meager supplies. When hunger begins to gnaw again, they kill and eat Juan's old spaniel, which he had rescued. Then they eat their leather caps and their shoes.

When they have been seven days in the longboat and no breeze has blown for four days, one of them whispers to his companion and the whisper goes from him to another and so all through the boat. They have decided that one of their number should be sacrificed for food. The lot falls on Pedrillo, Juan's tutor, who is thereupon bled to death. Almost all in the boat commit cannibalism except Juan and three or four others. Several of those who have partaken of human flesh drink sea water and go into convulsions. In spite of this, they might have cast lots again had they not succeeded in catching three sea birds and had it not rained for the first time since the ship sank. Later they have the good fortune to catch a turtle that is sleeping on the water.

At length, when only four are left alive, land appears but the coast is steep and rocky. The current and the prevailing wind carry the longboat swiftly toward land, and when they strike a reef the boat overturns. One of the four men is snatched away by a shark; two, unable to swim, drown; but Juan, with the help of the oar, is able to crawl up on the sand and there collapses, unconscious.

When Juan regains consciousness, the first object he sees is a lovely female face peering into his. With her is another young lady, and together they do what they can to restore his strength. After they have rubbed his cold limbs and covered him with a cape, they shelter him in a nearby cave.

The two ladies attend to Juan daily, and under their care he soon recovers his strength. The name of one is Haidée; the other, Zoe, is Haidée's maid. Haidée's father is Lambro, a Greek pirate, who has built a palatial home on the Aegean island on which Juan has been cast up.

Because Haidée's father would sell Juan as a slave, Haidée does not dare take him into her house to recuperate but keeps him in the cave and brings him clothing, furs for a couch, and a daily supply of food. When Juan has recovered his strength, Haidée gives him lessons in Greek, a language Juan knows nothing of, by pointing and repetition. Soon the two fall in love.

After Juan has stayed in the cave for a month, Lambro's fleet puts out to sea and Juan is able to leave his hideout and take daily walks with Haidée, in the meantime improving his Greek. During these walks their love for each other deepens. Soon Haidée's heart is hopelessly lost to Juan, until one night, under the stars

> By their own feelings hallowed and united,
>   Their priest was Solitude, and they were wed:
> And they were happy—for to their young eyes
> Each was an angel, and earth Paradise.
>
> (St. 204)

Commentary

Canto II is divided into five general parts: (1) a transitional beginning by means of Juan's seasickness; (2) the storm and shipwreck; (3) existence in a small boat after the ship has sunk; (4) Juan's arrival on an island in the Aegean Sea and the swift development of a secret love affair between him and Haidée, the only child of a wealthy Greek pirate, smuggler, and slave trader; and (5) a "philosophical" concluding section on love, conceived of as one of the main sources of both pain and pleasure in this world.

After the cynical comic brilliance and mocking commentary on marriage in Canto I, Canto II may disappoint some readers. Byron substitutes disaster at sea for disaster in marriage, but in the end brings the canto back to the main subject of Canto I, namely, love. In the interests of variety and unity, he might have ended Canto II with Stanza 110, where Juan, who has barely escaped with his life, falls unconscious on the shore of an island. As it is, Juan, whom we saw at the close of Canto I fleeing naked, a rather ridiculous figure, from one illicit love, is thrown, almost naked, into another illicit love, in the last part of Canto II. Juan remains pretty much unchanged; he has learned nothing from experience. There is no indication that he is in the slightest concerned with the possible disastrous effects of his new love, just as he had not concerned himself with the consequences of his first love. In this respect he is in the tradition of the classical Don Juan, who goes gaily from one love to another. Byron does not condemn him, although he had made him an object of laughter in Canto I; neither does he condone his conduct with Haidée. Although Juan and Haidée merely responded to the gravitational pull of physical compatibility, they had both been brought up Christians, as Byron is careful to tell us. Finding themselves in an occasion of sin, they had yielded to nature seemingly without a struggle. Byron, however, has his eye on the reader, especially the critic, who would be quick to charge him with immorality. He provides no suggestive details, and in Canto III he shows how the wages of sin is death for Haidée and serious injury for for Juan. Even with these precautions, he did not escape the charge of immorality. Robert Southey, the poet laureate, made him the leader of the Satanic school of poetry.

Byron's treatment of Haidée is quite different from his treatment of Donna Julia. He analyzes Julia's conduct with amused irony because she was a product of a sophisticated Christian society, and married besides. Haidée belongs to a more primitive society and is single. Byron explains her conduct by saying that she forgot her Christian principles in a crisis of love:

> And Haidée, being devout as well as fair,
> Had, doubtless, heard about the Stygian river,
> And Hell and Purgatory—but forgot
> Just in the very crisis she should not.
>
> (St. 193)

No doubt Byron feels that she is more entitled to our sympathy because she did not manipulate her conscience as Donna Julia had; she did not try to convince herself that her course of conduct was other than what it was. She didn't think at all, in fact, and so as a mirror of humanity is far less interesting than Donna Julia, for whom the reader can feel pity because she was trapped in a loveless marriage. Haidée's case was not at all similar. She had had suitors; while growing to womanhood she had rejected several, as Byron informs us in Stanza 128—and the field was still wide open. Byron seems to have forgotten these suitors and all they imply, when he writes in Stanza 190:

> Haidée spoke not of scruples, asked no vows,
> Nor offered any; she had never heard
> Of plight and promises to be a spouse,
> Or perils by a loving maid incurred;
> She was all which pure ignorance allows.

The shipwreck scenes are vivid and unforgettable, with something of the realism of the eighteenth-century novelist Tobias Smollett about them in addition to a seasoning of Byronic irony. Byron's chief source for his materials in this episode was a collection of shipwreck accounts, by men who had been involved in the incidents, edited by Sir J. G. Dalyell in 1812, entitled

Shipwrecks and Disasters at Sea, but he used other accounts too, including Captain Bligh's account of the mutiny on the *Bounty.* From these sources he got the cutting away of the masts to right the ship, the effort of the sailors to get at the liquor supply, some of the sailors lashing themselves in their hammocks, the dog, the cannibalism, the choice of a victim by drawing lots, bleeding the victim to give him an easy death, the rainshower, the capture of the sleeping turtle, and other details. A reviewer was quick to point out Byron's indebtedness.

Byron's picture of man in the shipwreck stanzas is one which on the whole is all too true. In such circumstances principle and reason are apt to vanish. What we miss in all this is compassion for poor miserable mankind, and Byron's occasional facetiousness is out of place and angered the reviewers. Artistically, the cannibalism incident may be a blemish. It is ugly and may have been put in to shock rather than to show how men may behave adrift in a small boat without provisions. To make it plausible Byron should have gone into much greater detail in showing how it came about. Cannibalism among shipwrecked men adrift in a small boat is so rare that the literary use of it demands an adequate background, including sufficient characterization of those who suggest it and commit it. Without this the element of probability is weakened.

The island idyll in Canto II in its realism and detailed description commands the reader's keenest interest. As a realistic presentation of a love affair between two young people whom we see gradually falling in love with each other, there is nothing quite so good as it in English literature before Byron. We are not simply told that Juan and Haidée fall in love with each other. We see the process taking place before our eyes.

CANTO III

Summary

After several stanzas on the subject of love, in which he concludes that love and marriage are incompatible, Byron returns to

Haidée and Juan. Her father's long-delayed return makes her
more imprudent. Having taken care of all his business, Lambro
returns to his island port, which is on the opposite side of the
island from his house. When he comes to the top of the hill over-
looking his house, he is surprised and annoyed to see that his
domestics, instead of being at work, are idling, dancing, and
feasting, and that guests are entertaining themselves and being
entertained. Having been out of contact with his home for some
time, Lambro could not know that a report of his death has come
to his island and that he has been mourned for several weeks.
The period of mourning over, Haidée and Juan have moved into
his home as man and wife, and entertain lavishly. The first fear
that enters the mind of the stern Lambro, whom the enslavement
of his country has made a formidable enemy of all mankind and
for whom Haidée is his sole bond with humanity, is that she has
betrayed him. He enters his house unseen by a private door, and
there in his main hall sit Juan and Haidée, surrounded by slaves
and feasting in the most luxurious surroundings on rare and cost-
ly food and drink. Haidée is dressed like a princess and radiantly
beautiful. Juan is likewise resplendently dressed.

At the moment they are being entertained by a famous poet,
a turncoat who will write verses in praise of any cause, provided
he is paid for it. The song that he sings for Haidée and Juan is a
lament for Greece's present state of subjection to Turkey and for
her lack of patriotic ardor, the famous "The Isles of Greece."

When the song is over Byron digresses on the subject of the
wide and lasting effect a poet's words may have and on the tran-
sitory nature of human fame. Great deeds owe more to the his-
torian than to the illusion called glory, and the biographer may
record acts that little redound to the glory of the one whose life
he is writing. At this point Byron devotes three stanzas to excori-
ating Southey, Wordsworth, and Coleridge, who have abandoned
their early liberalism for conservatism. He singles out Words-
worth's *Excursion*, "The Waggoner," and "Peter Bell" for spe-
cial ridicule. Byron now returns to his story but only to say that
Haidée and Juan's evening meal is over and to rhapsodize on the
beauty of the twilight which arouses in him a spirit of devotion.

His altars, he says, are the earth, the ocean, the stars, the air. With a paean on the charms of twilight Byron closes Canto III.

Commentary

Of chief interest in Canto III are the descriptions of food, dress, and furnishings and the character of Lambro. Although Byron does not refrain from making Lambro's way of making a living a target of his mockery, he characterizes the freebooter seriously and even makes something of a hero out of him. Lambro is a patriot in his own way; it is his bitterness about the present enslaved state of Greece that makes him an enemy of the world. He has in him the rudiments of ancient Greek culture in his taste for music, architecture, and beauty. His soured patriotism makes him a misanthrope, but he has a genuinely deep and tender love for his only child, Haidée. Thus when he comes back and finds that Haidée has practically forgotten him, the only spark of humaneness in him is extinguished.

Having brought Lambro into his palatial residence, Byron creates suspense by holding off the anticipated reunion of father and daughter by descriptions of clothing and viands, a patriotic interlude, cynical stanzas on the nature of fame, the perfidy and dullness of the Lake poets, the religious atmosphere of twilight, when the Angelus bell strikes—holds it off for fifty stanzas of *ottava rima* plus a lyric of sixteen six-line stanzas. Instead of creating suspense, Byron's digressions may make some readers forget that a story is being told.

Though the canto lacks action, it is far from being uninteresting. The rich descriptions of luxurious living, the characterization of Lambro, the plea for conquered Greece, the amusing attacks on the Lake poets, all make Canto III good, if not exciting, reading.

What may be regarded as a weakness in the canto is that while Byron provides realistic descriptions of things (partly borrowed from books), he makes little attempt to give an adequate account of his setting so far as the inhabitants are concerned: how many there were, what their relations to Lambro were, what contacts they had with other islands, what they thought of Haidée's living openly with the young Spanish stranger who had appeared from nowhere. Byron chooses to ignore all this; what doesn't interest him or what doesn't seem important to him he simply omits. Yet the canto would be a better one if he had included this material; it would bring the poem closer to the realistic novel, which in many ways it parallels. *Don Juan* and Henry Fielding's *Tom Jones* are related works. The reader could spare at least some of the concluding stanzas with their somewhat ill-natured blows at other poets for more development of the island background of Don Juan and Haidée's romance. The long introductory account of the turncoat poet (who is Robert Southey, the poet laureate, whom Byron makes mincemeat of in his "The Vision of Judgment") who sings "The Isles of Greece" could have been shortened, but Byron could not resist the temptation to use an opportunity to keep alive the long-standing feud with Southey.

CANTO IV

Summary

After seven stanzas in which he complains of the difficulty of making a beginning in poetry; confesses that his imagination is weakening; that the sad truth turns what was once romantic to burlesque ("And if I laugh at any mortal thing,/ 'Tis that I may not weep" — St. 4); admits that some have accused him of designs against "the creed and morals of the land"; and claims that his only intention is to be merry, Byron reintroduces Haidée and Juan. They were not meant to grow old but were meant to die in happy springtime. Whom the gods love die young. They think not of time's ravages; they find fault only with the way it speeds away from them. Their existence is a perfect one. They are like children, or like a nymph and her beloved, and are not meant to fill a place in a real world. They are perfectly happy.

This particular evening a tremor sweeps over them, they know not why, and a tear appears in Haidée's eye, but she dismisses the omen with a kiss when Juan questions her. Later, while they are taking their siesta, Haidée dreams that she is chained to a rock. Then in her dream she is released and begins to pursue something in a sheet which keeps eluding her. Her dream changes; she is in a cave and at her feet lies Juan lifeless. As she gazes, she thinks his features change into her father's. She awakes with a start and sees her father's eyes fixed on her and Juan. Shrieking, she arises and falls. Juan springs up at her shriek and grabs his saber off the wall. Lambro now speaks for the first time, scornfully commanding Juan to put away his foolish sword, for with a word he can summon a thousand scimitars. Haidée begs her father to spare Juan. Once more Lambro commands Juan to surrender his sword. When Juan refuses, Lambro draws his pistol and cocks it. Haidée then throws herself before Juan and begs her father to shoot her first. Her father replaces his pistol in its holster and blows a whistle. At once twenty of his men appear. With a quick movement Lambro grasps his daughter and pulls her away from before Juan. "Arrest or kill the Frank," he commands his men. The pirates push forward, and though Juan fights valiantly, wounding two of them, he is soon on the ground, bleeding from the arm and head. Lambro then gives his men orders to carry Juan to one of his ships.

When she sees Juan on the floor and bleeding, Haidée collapses in her father's arms and blood flows from her mouth from a vein which has burst. For several days she is in a coma. When she finally regains consciousness, she recognizes no one. The attendants try rousing her with harp music. The music succeeds in making her weep. She arises and flies at everyone in sight as at a foe. For twelve days she refuses food, clothing, and change of surroundings. On the twelfth day she dies, and with her dies Juan's unborn child, "a fair and sinless child of sin."

When Juan comes to, he finds that he is at sea, and a slave. With him are some fellow captives, an Italian opera company who had been on their way to Sicily and who have been sold into slavery by their impresario. Juan learns that he and his new friends are bound for the slave market in Constantinople.

Byron brings the canto to a close with the buffo's malicious description of the other members of the troupe, some remarks on fame, an appeal to his lady readers not to abandon him, and a brief description of the slave auction.

Commentary

Byron shows narrative skill in holding off his big scene in Canto IV as long as he reasonably can. In his seven introductory stanzas, besides commenting on a number of other matters, he prepares us for, while postponing, his major action, by giving us his opinion that it is better that the happy young should die while they are still young rather than that they should live on until they have lost their happiness and have to endure the miseries of aging. He is giving his readers a hint that Haidée is going to die. He can't, of course, let Don Juan die without bringing his story to an end. Then he uses two technical narrative devices to prepare us for the death of Haidée, namely, a feeling of foreboding and Haidée's ominously significant dream, from which she awakes to see the face of her father before her. Awaking from bad dreams usually brings relief; in Haidée's case consciousness brings her face to face with the father she thought was dead. The nightmare of her dreams becomes the much worse nightmare of actual fact. Her father has risen from the dead, so it seems to her, and knowing him she knows what will happen to Juan and to her happiness.

The effect on her is literally shattering. She has what is obviously a severe hemorrhage. The long postponed confrontation comes in a completely unexpected and dramatically effective way. It has to be admitted that Byron draws out the pathos of Haidée's ending, but he could say in his own defense that death is not ordinarily merciful and quick. In the father-daughter encounter Byron is careful to keep facetiousness to an absolute minimum. His instinct was right in telling him that here jokes were out of place. In the Haidée-Don Juan episode he created one of the great love stories of all time by description, skillful manipulation of action, and tight control of the comic vein that was part of the general design of *Don Juan*. When Byron writes, in ending Haidée's story, that ". . . no dirge, except the hollow sea's/ Mourns o'er the Beauty of the Cyclades" (St. 72), the reader is moved not only by the beauty of the words but by the fate of Byron's fictional "beauty of the Cyclades."

Byron again shows his realization of the emotional requirements of good storytelling when he turns almost abruptly from the pathos of Haidée's brief but happy experience of love to a sardonic description of the opera company whose treacherous impresario had sold them as a group into slavery. Island idylls are few and brief, Byron is telling his readers, but misfortune of one kind or another is the common lot of man and may be expected momentarily.

The contrast between Byron's briefly happy pair of lovers and the wretched group of singers and dancers is very effectively made with a minimum of characterization. Byron is very possibly enjoying a little bit of "getting even" for having been subjected to some poor musical performances during his Italian period. The prima donna looks haggard from dissipation. The tenor's wife has a mediocre voice. The dancers eke out their income by prostitution. One of them is a slut, one a spendthrift, and one a poor dancer. Among the other singers, the tenor's "voice is spoilt by affectation," the bass can only bellow, and the conceited baritone has a "voice of no great compass." Byron satirizes his characterizer by the name he gives him, Raucocanti, "hoarsesong." It is difficult for the reader to feel pity for their fate when the buffo is through with them.

CANTO V

Summary

In the slave market of Constantinople, Don Juan meets Johnson, an Englishman who had been a mercenary in the Russian army and who had been wounded and captured by the Turks.

Johnson freely tells Juan about his wife trouble, just as Byron would tell casual visitors about his own marital troubles. Johnson's first wife had died, his second wife had left him, and he had left the third. Juan tells Johnson that his present troubles are related to his having fallen in love.

The pair are bought by a black eunuch who brings them by boat to a palace. There he has Johnson dress as a Turkish gentleman and has Juan put on woman's garb. Juan objects and Baba, the eunuch, threatens. Four slaves then lead Johnson off to dinner, but Juan is commanded to follow Baba to an apartment in which a lady reclines under a canopy. The lady, Gulbeyaz, who is the sultan's fourth wife, dismisses her attendants. Baba tells Juan to kiss the sultana's foot, but Juan refuses. He "could not stoop/ To any shoe, unless it shod the Pope" (St. 102). Baba then proposes that Juan kiss her hand, and that he is willing to do. The sultana now dismisses Baba and addresses Juan. "Christian, canst thou love?" Her words bring the thought of Haidée to Juan's mind, and he bursts into tears.

Surprised by his tears, Gulbeyaz lays her hand on his and looks into his eyes but finds no sign of love there. Then she throws herself on Juan's breast, but Juan gently disengages himself. He tells her that he does not love her, that love is only for the free. His rejection of her embrace and his words surprise, humiliate, and anger her, and for a moment she thinks of killing him but instead begins to cry. Juan, who was prepared to die, regrets that he has hurt the beautiful young sultana and begins to "stammer some excuses." At this crucial moment Baba returns to announce that the sultan is coming to visit his favorite wife. The sultana's attendants are summoned, Juan joins them, and the sultan enters. The sultan notices the new lady-in-waiting and remarks that it is a pity that a mere Christian should be so pretty. The compliment draws all eyes to Juan. "There was a general whisper, toss, and wriggle" (St. 156), and the canto comes to an end with a promise by Byron that the sixth canto will "have a touch of the sublime."

Commentary

The fifth canto introduces a number of new characters into the story. Johnson, the English soldier of fortune, is a cheerful stoic and cynic. He believes that life brings only illusion and disappointment. Love, ambition, avarice, vengeance, glory only draw us on to folly. Johnson is, in part, Byron self-portraiture, but he is less prone to melancholy than Byron. He has a good sense of humor and is practical. Byron does not tell us why Baba buys him.

The other chief characters are Baba, the eunuch; Gulbeyaz, one of the sultan's wives, and the most beautiful of the four; and the sultan. Baba is a rather conventional character. He is the chief servant of the pampered Gulbeyaz and carries out her commands with prudence and efficiency. In Canto V he must cater to a whim of the sultana, which is to buy Don Juan, whom she had seen on his way to the slave market and whom she immediately wished to acquire. Byron amusingly makes Baba a proselytizer for Mohammedanism: he suggests to Johnson and Juan that they be circumcised, but he would leave the matter up to them. Johnson

> . . . thanking him for this excess
> Of goodness, in thus leaving them a voice
> In such a trifle, scarcely could express
> "Sufficiently" (he said) "his approbation
> Of all the customs of this polished nation.

> "For his own share—he saw but small objection
> To so respectable an ancient rite;
> And, after swallowing down a slight refection
> For which he owned a present appetite,
> He doubted not a few hours of reflection
> Would reconcile him to the business quite."
> (Sts. 70-71)

Juan is not so diplomatic as Johnson:

> "Will it?" said Juan, sharply: "Strike me dead,
> But they as soon shall circumcise my head!"
> (St. 71)

The sultan is of no special interest. He is merely an all-powerful Mohammedan potentate with a large harem and a large family who holds other people's lives cheap. Byron characterizes him satirically.

Gulbeyaz is, of course, the character of chief interest in the canto. She is a very special type of woman representing, in the society Byron knew, the wife who because of her means and power could buy herself a lover. Besides wealth and power she also has beauty and youth. She is twenty-six, just three years older than Donna Julia, and like Donna Julia she is love-starved and not disposed to remain so if she can help it. Not having had the experience of having her whims thwarted by anyone less than a sultan, she adopts the wrong approach to Don Juan: she commands him to be her lover. Juan can still be moved to tears by the memory of his lost Haidée, a fact which puts a barrier, at least a temporary one, between him and Gulbeyaz, and he has had no experience in being commanded to love by a queen. Besides, he has his pride. Donna Julia had seduced him, or at any rate encouraged him to seduce her; Haidée had won him from the sea, and she and Juan were on the same footing so far as youth, rank, and freedom to love were concerned; but being bought by a woman and told to love her, even though she is a beautiful young woman, arouses his stubbornness. Gulbeyaz uses the wrong technique, but because of her harem background she knows no other. Juan's proud refusal rouses her anger, and her frustration and shame reduce her to tears. Her tears move Juan to pity and are far more potent to overcome his will (not very strong when it came to women), than her commands. But the situation does not allow very much time. Gulbeyaz must act quickly, and the sultan's coming makes her gambit of no avail. She has loved and lost in a matter of minutes. Byron cleverly teases the reader by leading him to expect another affair and then abruptly shuts off the canto.

In Canto V Byron has moved his hero eastward into an entirely new environment out of which he may spin numerous stanzas and present a mode of life on which he may comment freely. In Canto V Byron is back in the mood with which the poem began, the mood of comic irony.

There is much that is entertaining in the canto. The admission in Stanza 4 of his love for the name of Mary reminds us that at sixteen Byron had fallen in love with Mary Chaworth and perhaps never quite recovered from the affair. The slave market is interestingly presented. The reader welcomes the appearance on the scene of Johnson, the practical accepter of life as it comes, who tells Juan (when the latter proposes that they knock out Baba and escape) that he is hungry and would like to eat first.

The stanzas (33-39) on the murder of a military commandant in Ravenna, which was brought to Byron's attention in the way he describes while he was living in Ravenna, tell us something about Byron's religious problems. The long walk through the sultan's palace; Byron's comments on how huge rooms and huge houses dwarf men; Juan's natural reluctance to don ladies' clothing and his transformation into a girl; the comment of Juan, who has shown no great piety, when told to kiss the sultana's foot that that act of homage was reserved for the pope; the interview between Gulbeyaz and Juan; and Byron's introduction of the sultan into the story, all contribute to make Canto V an interesting and amusing if not an exciting one.

CANTO VI

Summary

Canto VI is a continuation of the story of Juan in the harem. Since there is no bed available for Juan at the moment, the "Mother of the Maids," who is in charge of the harem, decides that "Juanna" will have to share the bed of Dudù, a pretty odalisque of seventeen. In the middle of the night, when all the harem is asleep, Dudù screams so loudly that she awakens all her companions, who hurry to see what is wrong. Dudù, with some embarrassment, explains that she dreamt that she was walking in a wood and came to a tree on which hung a golden apple. After she had tried in vain to get the apple, it fell down of its own accord at her feet. When she picked it up to bite into it, a bee flew out of it and stung her. At this point in her strange dream she awoke with a loud scream. Dudù is extremely apologetic for the disturbance she has caused, and the harem finally settles down to sleep again.

When the sultana awakes the following morning, she sends for Baba to find out what disposition has been made of Juan. Baba tries to keep the truth from her, but her close questioning forces him to confess that Juan has shared the couch of Dudù. When the sultana learns this, she is infuriated and commands Baba to summon the two and to prepare to dispose of them in the usual way: tie them in sacks and drop them into the sea. Baba tries to get her to change her mind, but he soon sees that she is inflexible.

Commentary

Canto VI is considerably less interesting than the preceding cantos. The story element is small, and the random comments on love and women slow down the pace to a crawl. That is not to say that the canto is dull. There is interest of some kind in every stanza that helps to make up for the dearth of narrative material. If the hundreds of stanzas of *Don Juan* may be compared to diamonds, there are none of them that do not have at least one good facet, a thought, a pun, a well expressed phrase or line, or an ingenious rhyme. The reader is entertained by Byron's skill in expressing himself, by what he has to say, and by the cleverness shown in finishing off a stanza with a witticism.

Byron's inventiveness seems to have failed him once he had decided to let Juan spend a night in the harem. His problem was to get him out of the harem and into the war episode he had promised his readers in Canto I, Stanza 200. An attack on war must have been part of his design in bringing Juan to Turkey, which had been at war with its neighbors off and on since the establishment of the Turkish Empire. It was too soon to have Juan involved in a third love affair, and so Byron used the convenient arrival of the sultan to break off his Gulbeyaz-Juan scene just when Juan was on the point of succumbing to the appeal to tears on the part of the sultana.

The dream sequence in Canto VI is innuendo of a not very subtle kind, and Dudu's dream of a golden apple out of which flies a bee that stings her is scarcely absorbing. Byron's Pegasus has slowed down to a walk. His customary cleverness has failed him in this instance, and Dudù's dream, while it may serve to wake up a harem, doesn't capture the reader's interest. It serves Byron's purpose, however, which is to get Juan out of the seraglio in a plausible way. Had Dudù not screamed, Gulbeyaz would have had no reason for getting rid of Juan. It got Byron off the hook. The question may be raised whether Gulbeyaz, who was in intention unfaithful to her fifty-nine-year-old husband and who had to share him with some fifteen hundred other women, would have condemned Juan to death on the suspicion that he was unfaithful to her when she had no claim on his affections. She had merely bought his person, not his fidelity or loyalty. The answer to this question may lie in the kind of character and personality Byron gives Gulbeyaz. She is a creature of whims and emotion who makes almost no use of her reason. She bought Juan to satisfy her lust; she condemns him to death to satisfy her craving for vengeance. It might not even occur to such a woman that a live Juan would serve her purposes even though he had fallen under suspicion of philandering.

In Canto VI Byron sacrificed an excellent opportunity to satirize the human phenomenon of polygamy. In *Don Juan* he satirizes any number of human failings, but in the case of the institution of the harem he confines himself to remarking that

> Polygamy may well be held in dread,
>   Not only as a sin, but as a *bore:*
> Most wise men with *one* moderate woman wed,
>   Will scarcely find philosophy for more;
> And all (except Mahometans) forbear
> To make the nuptial couch a "Bed of Ware."
>   (St. 12)

46

Instead of satirizing he sentimentalizes over his vision of fifteen hundred imprisoned beauties longing for love. (In Canto V the number is a thousand; in Canto VI Byron raised it to fifteen hundred.)

CANTO VII

Summary

Canto VII, one of the shortest in *Don Juan*, is primarily an introduction to Canto VIII, in which Byron describes the Battle of Ismail. In the first seven stanzas Byron defends himself against those critics of *Don Juan* who accuse the poet of "A tendency to under-rate and scoff/ At human power and virtue . . ." (St. 3). In holding up the nothingness of life he only does what writers like Solomon, Dante, Swift, and others have done. He laughs at all things, for all things are merely a show. He will now tell his readers about the siege of Ismail.

Ismail is a Turkish fortress at the mouth of the Danube, defensible against attack by land but not by water. The Russians arrive by water, set up their artillery on an islet in the Danube and begin firing on the city. When their cannonading does not bring about the surrender of the city, the commander of the Russian flotilla decides to withdraw. At this point a courier arrives with the news that Marshal Suvaroff (Suwarrow) has been put in command of the Russian troops.

The arrival of Marshal Suvaroff raises the spirits of the discouraged Russians. He immediately begins preparations for a fresh assault. He even teaches the raw recruits how to use the bayonet. He is everywhere, "Surveying, drilling, ordering, jesting, pondering" (St. 55).

In the midst of his preparations, some Cossack soldiers bring before him a group dressed in Turkish clothing. They are Don Juan, Johnson, a eunuch, and two women. Suvaroff knows Johnson by reputation and commands him to report to his old regiment. Juan is to serve with the marshal, and the women are sent to the baggage wagons. Meanwhile the work of preparation for an attack the following day goes on.

Commentary

The general background of Canto VII is one of the several wars waged between Russia and Turkey. During this war Catherine the Great was czarina of Russia. The immediate background is the siege and capture of a Turkish stronghold on the Danube, now part of Rumania, by one of Catherine's generals, Aleksandr Vasilievich Suvorov, in 1790. The details of the siege of Ismail Byron found in a French work, *An Essay on the Ancient and Modern History of New Russia,* by the Marquis Gabriel de Castelnau, as he acknowledged in the Preface to Cantos VI, VII, and VIII, which were published as one volume. The war ended with the defeat of the Turks by Russia.

The freshness of a new subject in *Don Juan* and Byron's strong feelings about war make Cantos VII and VIII two of the most absorbing and liveliest books in the poem. The most interesting character in Canto VII is, of course, General Suvorov, or Suwarrow, as Byron calls him, the Russian general whose chief achievements were his part in defeating the French Revolutionary armies in 1799 in northern Italy. Byron shows good narrative technique in introducing him dramatically in Stanza 43 just when the Russians, who had bungled the attack on Ismail, are about to retreat. The sixty-year-old general by word and example restores the sagging morale of the Russian troops. While Byron seems to admire the spirit and efficiency of Suvorov, he by no means idealizes him. He is "the greatest Chief/ That ever peopled Hell with heroes slain,/ Or plunged a province or a realm in grief" (St. 68). Suvorov is a professional soldier who cares little for human lives or women's tears. His business is leading armies, winning victories, and gaining glory. It makes little difference to him who the enemy is or whose blood is shed. Freedom means nothing to him.

Byron brings Don Juan back into the story in a similarly dramatic way in the middle of the canto on the day before

Suwarrow is to make his attack on Ismail. With him are Johnson, a eunuch, and two women. Byron does not bother telling the reader how Johnson and Don Juan got together again, nor how the party of five escaped from the harem. Nor does he identify the three companions of Juan and Johnson. The eunuch, however, is probably Baba, and one of the women may be Dudù. The other may be Lolah or Katinka, who might have offended the sultana by asking the Mother of the Maids to let Juanna share their beds (Canto VI, Sts. 47-49). Here once more Byron is teasing the reader and leaving him to his own devices. The eunuch and the two women are introduced into Canto VII and we never hear of them again.

Byron's sympathies in the canto are neither with the Russians, who are as interested in material gain as in defeating the infidel, nor with the Turks, but with those who are to be killed or wounded in the attack, and his scorn is for all who confuse glory and bloodshed. He is, he feels, presenting truth, an unwelcome and unpleasant commodity generally — when it concerns man's behavior. In all this he has time to play with the difficulty of pronouncing and spelling Russian names and to ridicule the blunders of Turks and Russians alike, to comment on the accidental nature of fame, man's bloodthirstiness, and to defend himself against his critics.

The last two stanzas, which soberly anticipate the slaughter of the morrow, make a very effective conclusion to the canto, and the line with which he ends, "The death-cry drowning in the Battle's roar" strike the keynote of Canto VIII.

CANTO VIII

Summary

The storming of Ismail begins with a Russian artillery barrage, which is soon answered from within the fortress. The Russian columns are ordered to attack and the slaughter commences. Instead of attempting to describe the battle in detail, Byron concentrates on the fortunes of Juan and Johnson, who are fighting in the same unit. They begin their march forward "dead bodies trampling o'er/ Firing, and thrusting, slashing, sweating, glowing," wallowing "in the bloody mire/ Of dead and dying thousands" (St. 19), sometimes gaining ground, sometimes being forced to yield ground. Byron's excuse for Juan's part in the attack is that he is a creature of impulse and is fascinated by the honor to be gained in battle. By chance Juan becomes separated from his unit. As he rushes along he finds himself in General Lascy's second column. Johnson, who had "retreated," makes a reappearance. Favored by accident and blunder they and their companions find themselves inside the walls of Ismail and Juan is commended by General Lascy himself. In spite of fierce resistance from the Turks, the Russian forces advance and succeed in closing in on the Turkish commander-in-chief, to whom they offer quarter. He refuses and is killed. The whole city is then captured but only part by part, for the Turks refuse to surrender:

> The bayonet pierces and the sabre cleaves,
>   And human lives are lavished everywhere,
> As the year closing whirls the scarlet leaves
>   When the stripped forest bows to the bleak air,
> And groans, and thus the peopled city grieves,
>   Shorn of its best and loveliest, and left bare;
> But still it falls in vast and awful splinters,
> As oaks blown down with all their thousand winters.
>   (St. 88)

Juan shows his humanity by saving the life of a Turkish girl of ten trying to hide in a pile of slaughtered women. Two Cossacks are about to put her to the sword when Juan arrives and by slashing the hip of one and the shoulder of the other saves the wounded little girl. When Juan insists that he will advance no farther until he has put the girl in a place of safety, Johnson commands a number of his followers to guard the girl.

Among the last of the Turks to yield are a Tartar Khan and his five sons. He rejects an opportunity to surrender and sees his sons killed one by one before his eyes. Even then he will not yield and joins his sons in death.

When the whole of the city is under the control of the Russians, crimes of every description are committed:

> All that the mind would shrink from of excesses —
> All that the body perpetrates of bad;
> All that we read — hear — dream, of man's distresses —
> All that the Devil would do if run stark mad;
> All that defies the worst which pen expresses, —
> All by which Hell is peopled, or as sad
> As Hell — mere mortals, who their power abuse —
> Was here (as heretofore and since) let loose.
>   (St. 123)

After the battle Suwarrow pens a message for Queen Catherine: "Glory to *God* and to the Empress! . . . Ismail's ours" (St. 133).

Commentary

In his attack on war and its false glory through his account of the capture of Ismail, Byron's general method is to stress the bloodshed and loss of life involved. The soldiers have to march over the bodies of the dead and wounded in order to advance; they must wallow "in the bloody mire/ Of dead and dying thousands" (St. 20). The Russians "fell as thick as harvests beneath hail,/ Grass before scythes, or corn before the sickle" (St. 43). They slide "knee-deep in lately frozen mud,/ Now thawed into a marsh of human blood" (St. 73). "The city's taken — only part by part — / And Death is drunk with gore" (St. 82). "Upon a taken bastion, where they lay/ Thousands of slaughtered men, a yet warm group/ Of murdered women . . ." (St. 91) may be seen. ". . . the glow/ Of burning streets like moonlight on the water,/ Was imaged back in blood, the sea of slaughter" (St. 122).

In addition to showing the horrors of war, Byron subjects war to a continuous blistering attack of satirical comment. The combination of the two methods is calculated to make the reader strongly anti-war. War is hell, says Byron. Here he becomes involved in a dilemma, because he defends wars of liberation, wars in defense of freedom. (Sts. 4-5) If war is hell, there can be no exception, for in wars in defense of liberty as much blood may be spilled as in wars of aggression. The dilemma is inescapable when war is condemned by showing its horrors. The battles fought by Leonidas and Washington (St. 5) can result in as much bloodshed as battles fought by tyrants.

Even though Byron does not escape from the dilemma in which his vividly concrete and hyperbolical method of condemning war involves him, he shows that war is not all horror by having Don Juan save the life of a ten-year-old Turkish girl by the somewhat incongruous method of wounding two of his allies in the process. Furthermore, quarter is offered to the enemy by the Russians on more than one occasion.

Byron, on the whole, is sympathetic toward his very human and imperfect hero, Don Juan. Why then does he allow Juan to commit the major crime of enthusiastically waging war against the inhabitants of a city that had done him no injury? Byron does not excuse him; he makes sarcastic comments on his behavior in Stanzas 24 and 25, calling his valor "a thing of impulse." It might be added that Juan as killer is a victim of the plot of *Don Juan*, in which, among many other things, Byron wants to attack war — specifically, aggressive war.

Byron himself becomes a victim of the "noble savage" legend of the eighteenth century in Stanzas 61-67 of Canto VIII. In these stanzas he digresses to deliver a panegyric on Daniel Boone, whose fame had come to his ears. Daniel, he says, was the happiest of mortals who, killing nothing but a buck or bear, spent "the lonely, vigorous, harmless days/ Of his old age in wilds of deepest maze" (St. 61). Byron says nothing or knows nothing of the number of Indians that Boone had killed in his time. To Byron, Boone was not the only one of his kind, for around him grew up a race of tall, strong, cheerful, incorrupt people of the woods. But the poet does not mention that Boone and his followers took, by force, the place of another incorrupt people of the woods. He ignores this fact, and boldly asserts that these kindly folk are the product of Nature. What goes on at Ismail is the product of Civilization. (St. 68).

CANTO IX

Summary

The first ten stanzas are an attack on Wellington, who has
won the Battle of Waterloo and has been richly rewarded by
England for his victory. He should not have accepted the gifts
his country lavished on him, Byron thinks; he should have been
satisfied with thanks, like Epaminondas, who saved Thebes, and
Washington, who freed his country. He could have freed Europe
from the tyrannical kings who rule her and he did not. "Never
had mortal man such opportunity, Except Napoleon, or abused
it more" (St. 9).

Returning to the narration, we find that Don Juan has been
chosen by Suwarrow to carry the news of the capture of Ismail to
the Empress Catherine in Petersburgh. As he kneels before the
queen with his dispatch, his youthful good looks make such an
impression on her that for some moments she forgets to break the
seal. She falls in love with him even as she gazes on him. Then
she opens the dispatch and "great joy is hers."

The attention of the whole court is drawn to Juan when they
see that he has won the favor of the empress. Catherine's love
for Juan is returned. Although she is much older than he is, "he
was of that delighted age/ Which makes all female ages equal"
(St. 69).

Commentary

The attack on England's military savior, prompted by
Byron's subject matter in Canto VIII, seems both strange as well
as intemperate and ungrateful. Byron was a Whig, a liberal, and
Wellington was a Tory. His feeling toward Wellington was rooted
in politics, but went beyond mere party differences. Wellington
had thrown his great influence on the side of the *status quo* and
reaction, and for Byron that meant an alliance with tyranny, an
attack on freedom.

The attack on a man who had saved his country from defeat by Napoleon, no matter what else he may or may not have done, shows a pettiness and lack of sense of propriety on Byron's part. Byron is altogether too eager to show that he is not a flatterer (St. 5), but there is genuine indignation present too.

Canto IX is more of a patchwork than any previous canto and contains less narrative. From Wellington Byron turns to the subject of death, which laughs at man, and to the impossibility of arriving at certitude about life. He turns to the subject of his politics: he wishes men to be free of any kind of tyranny, of mobs as well as of kings. And so he rambles on, as he says (St. 42) "now and then narrating,/ Now pondering. . . ." There is not much narrating, but Juan finally arrives in Petersburgh, the capital of Russia, with his ten-year-old Turkish orphan. Juan is himself about seventeen or eighteen.

Byron makes Catherine the Great seem much younger than she was. He speaks of "Her prime of life, just now in juicy vigour" (St. 72). In 1790, when Ismail was taken, Catherine, born in 1729, would be sixty-one and hardly in the prime of life; she died in 1796. Byron has to make her seem much younger than she is in order to make Juan one of her succession of lovers. Juan had, after all, refused a beautiful sultana of twenty-six. Byron knows how old Catherine really is, as he shows in Canto VIII, Stanza 88.

Byron, who is interested in Catherine mainly for Juan's sake, completely fails to do justice to her powerful personality, will, and intellect. If he had done as much for Catherine as he had for Marshal Suvorov, Canto IX would be much more interesting than it is.

CANTO X

Summary

In Russia Juan becomes a polished Russian courtier and in the process also becomes a little dissipated. He lives "in a hurry/

Of waste, and haste, and glare, and gloss, and glitter" (St. 26).
He writes to relatives in Spain about his present circumstances.
They answer promptly, impressed by his good fortune. A number
of them prepare to emigrate to Russia. His mother writes that she
has remarried and Juan now has a baby brother. She gives him a
lot of good advice on how to conduct himself in Russia.

Life in Russia, however, does not continue to agree with
Juan. He falls sick. The physicians, unable to determine the
exact cause of his illness, recommend a change of climate. It
happens that at the time the Empress Catherine is involved in
negotiations with the English and decides that Juan will handle
them. With his ward Leila and an entourage of valets and secre-
taries, he sets out across Europe, passing through Poland, Ger-
many, and Holland. Eventually the party arrives in London.

Their arrival in England is an invitation to Byron to make
some scathing remarks about his native land, whose sons have
"butchered half the earth, and bullied t'other" (St. 81). He ends
the canto with a promise of telling his fellow countrymen some
unpleasant truths about themselves which, he says, they will
not believe.

Commentary

Canto X is as devoid of narrative or incident as Canto IX, nor
does Byron make up for dearth of incident by introducing an
interesting character, as he had done in Canto VII in the person
of General Suvorov. There is, however, an abundance of lively
comment on a multitude of matters, and in Stanza 41 Byron per-
forms a tour de force in turning a prescription with all its medical
Latin and symbols into rhyme, a paraphrase of which can be
found in the fourth volume of the Steffan-Pratt variorum edition
of Don Juan.

England was hardly the country for a man who falls ill be-
cause of the rigors of the Russian climate. Spain would have been
much better, but Byron had obviously decided that he was going
to use Don Juan to satirize the country and the class that had

ostracized him. Byron devotes the last six cantos of his poem to this task. Possibly it was for this reason that Byron carried Don Juan to Russia, which Byron had never visited. His own travels had brought him only as far as Turkey, Russia's neighbor. In addition to enabling him to introduce Catherine the Great, one of the most colorful figures of the eighteenth century, into his poem, it enabled him to spin out some stanzas on courts and courtiers, which in his mind were synonymous with depravity, waste, venality, and every form of corruption. Putting Don Juan in a court atmosphere, moreover, helped to prepare him for living in high aristocratic circles in England. The Russian court helped to mature Juan, gave him poise and knowledge of the ways of the upper-class world. Juan arrived in Russia a boy and left it as a self-assured young man. Juan had also arrived at Ismail penniless, and if Byron at this time planned to send him to England to circulate in high society, he had to have money. So he sent him to the generous Catherine, who gave him a fortune. He came to England "rich in rubles, diamonds, cash, and credit" (St. 70). A Don Juan without wealth would have been a figure of very limited interest and influence in the fashionable society of England where there was no Catherine to make him her favorite. No aristocrat knew the value of money better than Byron, who was always having trouble with it.

CANTO XI

Summary

Don Juan gets out of his carriage and walks behind it in order to get a general view of London. As he meditates on what a law-abiding city London is, a knife is flashed in his face and a voice cries, "Your money or your life." Impulsively, he draws his pistol and mortally wounds the robber. This is Juan's introduction to life in England.

After he settles down and presents his credentials in the proper places, Juan is accepted by the class of society to which he belongs by birth. He becomes an object of romantic interest to unmarried and married young ladies. The bluestockings want to talk about literature with him. At parties large and small he meets the leading English writers of the time. He devotes his mornings to business, his afternoons to visits and luncheons, and his evenings to going to parties. As a young, rich, and handsome noble, Juan is very much in demand.

Commentary

There is little action in Canto XI and a great deal of satirizing. Byron's main purpose in placing Don Juan in the aristocratic world of early nineteenth-century England is to expose the shallowness, hypocrisy, and self-interest of that world. There is no genuine virtue in this society; there is only the appearance of virtue, according to Byron. It is interested in young men of Juan's class only for the sake of what it may get out of them. In the canto Byron's main purpose is to give a general, unfavorable, picture of this society and so let the readers of *Don Juan* know what perils their hero is exposed to. Later, he will concern himself with action and character. The broad outline is given first; the details will come later. Byron effectively establishes the tone of his social analysis at the beginning of the canto by having Juan held up by a robber with a knife just as Juan is meditating on how much virtue there must be in so vast a city as London. Even though it seems rather unlikely that Juan should look down on London from Shooter's Hill with such thoughts in his mind, the ironic incident serves its purpose very well. Juan's illusions are promptly shattered. He will not be deceived by appearances again during his sojourn in England.

Byron's purpose in having Juan mortally wound the would-be robber may be to keep Juan a realistic character and not let him become a mere device to achieve a piece of dramatic irony. Juan is prompt to act in war and love; his act of shooting Tom is characteristic of him; so too is his wish that "he had been less hasty with his flint" (St. 14) and his wish to help the wounded robber to his feet. It is also characteristic of Byron that he should expand the incident into ten stanzas and use it to show off his knowledge of low-life slang.

In demonstrating that Juan is well received in England be-
cause he is a foreigner of rank—young, handsome, and accom-
plished—Byron ridicules the bluestockings, a name given to
women who were, or affected to be, interested in learning and
literature. They were a favorite target of Byron's satire.

> Juan, who was a little superficial,
>   And not in literature a great Drawcansir,
> Examined by his learnéd and especial
>   Jury of matrons, scarce knew what to answer:
> His duties warlike, loving or official,
>   His steady application as a dancer,
> Had kept him from the brink of Hippocrene,
> Which now he found was blue instead of green.
>   (St. 51)

Juan got out of his literary difficulties by replying at random
"with/ A modest confidence and calm assurance" (St. 52). In
addition,

> Juan knew several languages—as well
>   He might—and brought them up with skill, in time
> To save his fame with each accomplished belle,
>   Who still regretted that he did not rhyme.
>   (St. 53)

The bluestockings, Byron implies, are shallow and easily taken
in by a superficial parade of knowledge that is not apropos.

The English poets of the time are also swept into Byron's
satirical net. Southey receives one more blow, and Keats, the
reader is told, "was killed off by one critique" (St. 60). In bring-
ing up the subject of other poets, Byron grows truculent and
promises that if he were in England and "in good satire" he
would show up the long list of pretenders to poetry. While Byron
is devoting nine stanzas to his fellow poets, Don Juan is tem-
porarily shelved.

A third block of stanzas in Canto XI is 76-85, in which Byron
develops his own variation of the "Where are the snows of
yesteryear?" theme. Byron is looking back over a period of eight

years, and in five stanzas beginning with the word "Where" he asks what has become of various persons, some known to history, like Napoleon, others known only to Byron, the friends or associates of earlier years. All have changed, not for the better, or have died. In the last three stanzas of this section of the canto, each of which begins with the words "I have seen" Byron reports other changes that have occurred, none of them good. The section ends with a piece of cynical advice to Don Juan: *Carpe diem,* get all you can out of each day in the way of pleasure and profit for you.

CANTO XII

Summary

Canto XII begins with a fourteen-stanza meditation on the misery of middle age (Byron is now thirty-five, he tells the reader in Stanza 2) and the pleasures of money, which Byron ironically sings the praises of. Money rules the world and even rules love. This meditation is followed by a boast about his youthful success as a writer and literary lion, of which he has lately paid the penalty, a comment on the passing nature of fame, and a tongue-in-cheek plea for procreation, which the Malthusians are currently opposed to.

In Stanza 23 he turns to Juan, at least by name, but it is Juan's ward Leila he takes up. The dowagers in Juan's set have decided that her education had better be taken out of Juan's management and put into that of one of themselves. At this point Byron stops to devote a few amusing stanzas to the young "fortune" who has just made her debut and the stir made about her by other females who wish to arrange a match for her with one of their relatives. This is followed by the admission that the lady who got *him* (Byron) didn't do so well.

Finally Lady Pinchbeck is chosen by Juan as a guardian for Leila. The author agrees that she is a good choice. She knows the world, she is witty, and her reputation is now safe.

Olden she was — but had been very young;
Virtuous she was — and had been, I believe.

(St. 43)

Once again Byron returns to Juan and then leaves him to descant upon the perils of high society for a young unmarried man. If he talks six times with the same single lady, her brother wants to know what his intentions are, and soon he is married. Then there are perils from the coquette, and from the wife who merely wants to be friendly. Such friendships end in lawsuits in England; abroad the consequences are less serious.

But Juan is no novice, and furthermore he is somewhat tired of love. And at first he didn't find the English women pretty. Here Byron stops to analyze the English woman. She has some ice in her and hides half her attractions. She glides into the heart and once there holds on. She does not have as many external graces as the Continental woman, nor is she quite so ready with her smile, but when she is taken with a *grande passion,* it is a very serious thing indeed, and if there is a disaster she is cast out by society and will not be allowed to return.

Commentary

Canto XII is, on the whole, amusing and no earlier canto is more brilliantly written. Byron is at his poetic best here; the stanzas flow on with the smoothness of a wide river. There is no faltering or stumbling. The rhymes are as smooth as ever and the expression nowhere superior in the whole poem. Whatever subject Byron takes up, and in this canto he takes up quite a number, he has something worth reading to say about it. In spite of the diversity of topics, the canto has a unity of theme — not Don Juan, for he is almost left out altogether — but the English woman of high society. In talking of her Byron is politely cynical and avoids sentimentalism scrupulously. He writes as the uninvolved, experienced commentator who understands the ways and wiles of English woman. In Canto XII and the remaining cantos Byron is more at home with his subject.

CANTO XIII

Summary

Among the friends made by Don Juan are Lord Henry Amundeville and his wife Lady Adeline. Lady Adeline is high-born, wealthy in her own right, and beautiful. She is

> The fair most fatal Juan ever met,
>> Although she was not evil nor meant ill;
> But Destiny and Passion spread the net
>> (Fate is a good excuse for our own will),
> And caught them. . . .

(St. 12)

She is chaste, enjoys a good reputation, and gets along well with her husband. She is polite to all; she has a calm patrician polish in her manner that checks rash enthusiasm. But she is not indifferent; like a volcano, she has heat within.

Her husband, Lord Henry, is reserved, cautious, proud, and discerning when it comes to judging people. He is a great debater in the House of Lords and thinks of himself as being well informed politically. He is a patriot and at the same time knows how to provide for himself.

Like all members of the aristocracy, the Amundevilles have a town residence and a country house. At the end of the winter season they leave London for their country mansion, Norman Abbey, the "Gothic Babel of a thousand years" (St. 50). Norman Abbey was once a monastery. Only one wall of the original Gothic church remains. Norman Abbey lies in a valley, above which are woodlands full of game. There is a lake in front of the mansion. In the court there is a Gothic fountain. Inside, there are "Huge halls, long galleries, spacious chambers" (St. 67), in which hang portraits of eminent Amundevilles as well as works by Titian, Rembrandt, Caravaggio, and other famous painters.

When September comes the Amundevilles invite to Norman Abbey for the hunting season a large group of friends and acquaintances, among them the Countess Crabby, Lady Scilly, Miss O'Tabby, the Duke of Dash, General Fireface, Sir Henry Silvercup, and Don Juan.

The great event of the day is dinner. Until that event comes the guests are left to themselves to fight off boredom as best they can. The young and middle-aged men engage in hunting and shooting, and the elderly spend their time turning over books in the library, walking in the gardens, reading the paper, or horseback riding. The women take walks, ride, read, write letters, sing, or practice the latest dance.

Commentary

Juan has no part in Canto XIII; he is mentioned only by name and in connection with Lady Adeline. Byron hints that an affair will develop between them (St. 12). In Canto XIII Byron gives the reader the setting for the affair hinted at and at the same time satirizes the English upper classes. The canto falls into five well defined parts, two of which are detailed characterizations of Lord Henry and Lady Adeline. Lady Adeline has been called the most complex character created by Byron up to this point in his literary career. The claim is well justified. The characterization of Lady Adeline alone would make the canto one of the best in the poem.

The third part of the canto, the description of Norman Abbey, to which Byron devotes seventeen stanzas, is a loving and nostalgic description of his own baronial home, Newstead Abbey, which he had sold in 1818, having decided at that time that he would never again live in England. The description of Norman Abbey fits Newstead Abbey, even down to the statue of the Virgin and Child in a niche of the facade which is the sole remnant of the medieval abbey church. The facade with its "grand arch," which was once a stained glass window, and the Blessed Virgin in her niche are still parts of Newstead Abbey.

The characterizations which form the fourth part of the canto are caricatures in the tradition of Restoration and eighteenth-century satire. Byron even mentions Congreve, the best of the Restoration comic dramatists, and he alludes to Fielding, the greatest of the eighteenth-century satirical novelists, in the canto. Byron's caricatures compare favorably with those of his models in brevity and pungency.

The last part of the canto wittily and cleverly describes the day's activities of the Amundevilles' guests and the difficulties they experience in getting through a day in the country.

Canto XIII, although it is devoid of narrative, is rich in good characterization and for that reason alone is one of the best cantos in *Don Juan*. The admirable structure of the canto reduces a large mass of varied material to an ordered sequence that makes the canto a pleasure to read. Digression is kept to a minimum. We must accept digression in *Don Juan* because it is an essential part of Byron's design, but random thoughts, though given a witty and striking form, are of less interest than good narrative and memorable characters.

CANTO XIV

Summary

Canto XIV begins with some "editorializing" on Byron's part. Man has no certainties in life, a fact which is proved by the proliferation of philosophical systems, which contradict each other. But what is the purpose of these skeptical speculations, he hears the reader ask him. His only excuse is, he answers, it's his way. He writes poetry as a form of play. The narrative in this poem, he says, is actually just a catch-all device. There is pleasure in publishing for him; it's a form of gambling. There is pleasure in waiting to see if the work is going to succeed or not. In addition, Byron says, what he publishes is of value to society, for he deals in facts, not fiction. It is an exposure of the hypocrisy, dullness, and boredom of high society. Following these stanzas is a set on women, whose lot, at best, Byron asserts, is an unhappy one.

With Stanza 31 Byron proceeds with his narrative. Juan in his new environment is a very adaptable young man and gets along well with all sorts of people:

> Born with that happy soul which seldom faints,
> And mingling modestly in toils or sports."
> (St. 31)

In fox hunting he shows a natural skill and conducts himself in such a way as to win the admiration of all. In conversation he remains alert, is a lively talker and a good listener. He avoids argument and humors the group he is a part of:

> Now grave, now gay, but never dull or pert;
> And smiling but in secret — cunning rogue.
> (St. 37)

He is an excellent dancer. It is no marvel that he is a general favorite:

> A full-grown Cupid, very much admired;
> A little spoilt, but by no means so quite;
> At least he kept his vanity retired.
> (St. 41)

The women among the company show special interest in him. One of them is the Duchess Fitz-Fulke,

> . . . a fine and somewhat full-blown blonde,
> Desirable, distinguished, celebrated
> For several winters in the grand, *grand Monde:*
> (St. 42)

where she has been the heroine of a number of exploits which the narrator could tell but won't. Currently, she has an admirer in Lord Augustus Fitz-Plantagenet. Her husband is not in the present company; in fact, she and the duke get along by keeping out of each other's way.

> Theirs was that best of unions, past all doubt,
> Which never meets, and therefore can't fall out.
> (St. 45)

It disturbs her good friend Lady Adeline greatly to see the duchess showing so much interest in Don Juan, or as Byron puts it, "to see her friend's fragility." She is also disturbed for Juan's sake, Byron says ironically; his inexperience moves her to pity. She is forty days older than he is; they are both twenty-one. (Sts. 42 and 44)

Lady Adeline therefore resolves to take such measures as are necessary. She is not concerned about the duke's making trouble; she is afraid the duchess will succeed and that she will have a quarrel with Lord Fitz-Plantagenet, who is aware of what is going on. So Lady Adeline consults with her husband, but his comments are not very helpful: he never interferes in anyone's business but the king's; he never judges from appearances; Juan is no fool and good rarely comes from good advice. He advises his wife to leave the parties to themselves. Having said this, he goes into his office — he is a member of the Privy Council — and as he leaves he calmly kisses his wife, "Less like a young wife than an agèd sister" (St. 69). Lord Henry is "a cold, good, honourable man" who, Byron says, lacks *soul* or an indefinable *je ne sais quoi.*

As for Adeline, belonging to high society she does not have enough to do. "Her heart was vacant, though a splendid mansion" (St. 85). She loves her Lord Henry, of course, but that love costs her an effort; at least she *thinks* she loves him. There is considerable disparity of temperament between them. Adeline is not easily impressionable, but once she identifies herself with some object, she will be carried away. Byron hints that the object may be Don Juan. "She knows not her own heart" (St. 91), and she has never really been in love. But Byron does not want the reader to make rash assumptions and warns him not to take it for granted that there will be an affair between Juan and Adeline. It's doubtful that Byron planned his story line very carefully in composing *Don Juan;* he seems to have relied on the spur of the moment. In Canto XIII, Stanza 12, he promised the reader that there would be an affair between Juan and Adeline. Later, he seems to have changed his mind, and in Canto XIV, Stanza 99, he warns the reader not to assume that there will be an affair between the two:

Above all, I beg all men to forbear
  Anticipating aught about the matter:
They'll only make mistakes about the fair,
  And Juan, too, especially the latter.
And I shall take a much more serious air
  Than I have yet done, in this Epic Satire.
It is not clear that Adeline and Juan
Will fall; but if they do, 't will be their ruin.

Commentary

Byron sketches a situation and amplifies characterization in Canto XIV. There is Lady Fitz-Fulke, the mischief maker, an intriguante, who is out to trap Juan. Opposed to her is Adeline, who is eager to save Juan from the duchess and who is, of course, as Byron makes clear enough by innuendo, in danger of falling in love with Juan. Adeline is a kind of English Donna Julia. She is not the wife of a man who is more than twice her age, but she is married to a husband who is cold by nature and who is more interested in business than he is in her. She has a child, but her child is not enough to occupy her time. She is idle, lacks an object in life. The elegant high society she lives in encourages idleness in its women. She is frustrated without quite realizing it.

Lady Adeline is a more complex figure than Donna Julia and less passionate, but like Donna Julia, she is presented as a woman who does not know herself and who is going to rationalize. She and Donna Julia are sisters under the skin, deprived of satisfaction in the life of the affections, and not really willing to discipline themselves. But first they must find reasons for doing what they are going to do anyway. Donna Julia lived in quite different circumstances; she did not move in the same kind of society as Lady Adeline. Although she belonged to the aristocracy, it does not seem to have been a very active aristocracy. Lady Adeline lives in an active society which she understands very well and which she can cope with. She is, in a way, a political figure in that her husband is a political figure. In this society she has a rival, whereas Julia had none, and that rival is at the present time her guest. As a character, she is more interesting, because less simple, than Donna Julia.

In Canto XIV the reader gets the first indication he has had of Juan's age since he left home at sixteen or seventeen. He was sixteen when he and Donna Julia fell in love. We are not told how many months have passed since that time and the time he embarks on the *Trinidada*. Obviously, we are to think of him as having been away from home between four and five years, since he is now twenty-one (Sts. 52 and 54). His mother intended him to be away four years altogether. Chronology doesn't mean much to Byron in *Don Juan*. Juan is twenty-one in England and that is all we need to know. Byron wants him to be twenty-one; he doesn't want to show us how he got to be twenty-one. As he says in stanza 54, "My Muse despises reference. . . ." We don't know how much time he spent on the island in the Cyclades or in Russia. Juan has not merely grown older; he has matured (Sts. 31-41).

In Canto XIV for the first time Byron uses his hero Don Juan as an agent of satire. When Byron tells us that Juan smiles "in secret—cunning rogue!" at something that has been said, as he does in stanza 38, Juan is outside of his society and superior to it. Up to this point Don Juan has been identified with his society and is satirized with that society. In Russia, for instance, he is not superior to Russian society nor does he seem to see the weakness of it. In Russia he is corrupted by a corrupt environment.

CANTO XV

Summary

After five stanzas on the author's poor opinion of life, Byron provides some more characterization of Don Juan, or at least reinforces what he had already provided. Juan's manner is natural; he makes no attempt to make an impression. There is nothing studied or artificial in his conduct. He is without pretense and his demeanor suggests sincerity. There is gentleness about him that attracts and that wards off suspicion. There is even a certain aloofness about him. He is serene, accomplished, cheerful, quiet, observant, and self-confident. Such are the personality and character of Don Juan at the age of twenty-one. He is obviously a source of danger to the prudent Lady Adeline, who wouldn't spare a look for an ogling, handsome dandy or a sophisticated seducer. The appearance of virtue in a Don Juan is her chief enemy; she is "no deep judge of character," and she is apt to transfer what is good in her own character to a man she feels attracted to.

> 'Tis thus the Good will amiably err,
> And eke the Wise, as has been often shown.

After his characterization of Don Juan, Byron stops to deliver some apology for what he is doing. He confesses he has no high aim or art:

> And never straining hard to versify,
> I rattle on exactly as I'd talk
> With anybody in a ride or walk."
>
> (St. 19)

He claims at least

> . . . a conversational facility,
> Which may round off an hour upon a time.
>
> (St. 20)

But he has his pride and independence; he will not court the critics and so writes as he does. If he wanted to please them, he would be more comic. But he was born for opposition; he cannot help being on the side of the underdog, and he would not have written poetry at all if someone (Henry Brougham in the *Edinburgh Review*, reviewing Byron's *Hours of Idleness*, advised the author to abandon poetry) had not told him *not* to write verse. He also has a difficult task, namely, to give a natural picture of manners that are artificial.

Having explained his poetic manner and task, Byron returns to Adeline, but he soon feels that he must generalize upon the particular. Adeline decides that, if Juan's soul is to be saved, he must marry. That calls for several ironic comments on matchmaking and the ironies of the married state. Adeline suggests several good matches, including Miss Millpond, "smooth as summer's sea," an obvious, sarcastic reference to the Miss Milbanke who become Lady Byron.

One good prospect whom Adeline does not mention, a fact which puzzles Don Juan, is the sixteen-year-old Aurora Raby. She is a Catholic, an orphan, wealthy, noble, pious, and virtuous. Byron contrasts her with Haidée, the product of nature rather than of society:

> . . . the difference in them
> Was such as lies between a flower and gem.
>
> (St. 58)

She is a perfect creature in a generally corrupt society. She has become what she is in spite of that society.

The marriage conference between Adeline and Juan terminates indecisively, brought to an end by the sound of the dinner bell. The dinner menu is described in some detail.

Juan is placed, "by some odd chance," between Aurora and Lady Adeline. Aurora, for some reason that Byron pretends not to know, pays little attention to Juan's gay conversation. Her aloofness causes Juan to exert himself all the more, and he finally succeeds in arousing her interest. Juan "had the art of drawing people out," (St. 82) and, "then he had good looks" (St. 84).

The canto concludes with the author's promise that a ghost will be introduced in the following canto.

Commentary

In Canto XV narrative interest is maintained by Adeline's determination to get Juan married. Byron does not explain exactly why Adeline wants Juan married, but in his characterization of Adeline he has given enough hints for the reader to draw his own conclusions. Adeline may not even be aware of the reasons herself. She cannot marry Juan herself but she may be able to marry him to one of a carefully selected list of young ladies over whom she could exercise some control and so keep up a special relationship of a kind she would never admit, even to herself. Aurora Raby is not in that list because Adeline knows instinctively that she could exercise no control over Aurora.

In the character of Aurora (Aurora was the Roman goddess of the dawn; the name connotes the freshness and purity of the dawn) Byron creates one of the most interesting of the *dramatis personae* of *Don Juan*. Byron gives a touch of pathos to his bright candle lit in a naughty world:

> Early in years, and yet more infantine
>   In figure, she had something of Sublime
> In eyes which sadly shone, as Seraphs' shine.
>   All Youth — but with an aspect beyond Time;
>   Radiant and grave — as pitying Man's decline;
>   Mournful — but mournful of another's crime,
>   She looked as if she sat by Eden's door,
>   And grieved for those who could return no more.
>   (St. 45)

She is a kind of sad seraph mourning for man's fall, for his irrevocable exclusion from the Garden of Paradise, for the sin that came into the world with the Fall. She is also a figure by which the world in which she moves by birth and position can be judged, she is in such contrast to it. She is the Ideal to its Real:

> She gazed upon a World she scarcely knew,
>   As seeking not to know it; silent, lone,
> As grows a flower, thus quietly she grew,
>   And kept her heart serene within its zone.
> There was awe in the homage which she drew;
>   Her Spirit seemed as seated on a throne
> Apart from the surrounding world, and strong
> In its own strength — most strange in one so young!
>   (St. 47)

Working together with Byron's mockery, she exposes Regency high society. One may ask whether she is not elevated above all nature. One answer to such a question is that there is the touch of nature in her that makes her susceptible to Juan's charm. The reader may wonder, however, what such a woman, married and a mother, would have done in such a society. Would she have remained aloof by necessity and so without influence, or, being what she was, could she have acted as a leavening force?

In Canto III Byron describes the hundred-dish Oriental dinner menu of Don Juan, Haidée, and their guests in two stanzas (62 and 63). In Canto XV he devotes thirteen stanzas to the Amundeville dinner menu. The menu versified is among the more interesting bits of miscellanea in *Don Juan*. No doubt Byron felt proud of his little tour de force here.

In devoting the concluding stanzas of the canto to the ghost he is going to introduce, Byron shows that he is not indifferent to the requisites of good narrative. His announcement of the ghost to come and his insistence that the existence of ghosts cannot be cavalierly dismissed, since we know so little about this world and nothing about the next, is a good suspense device.

CANTO XVI

Summary

Canto XVI is divided into four sections. The first section is a ghost episode. On the night of the great supper, Juan, after he has gone to bed, feels "restless, and perplexed, and compromised." His mind is filled with thoughts of the sixteen-year-old Aurora and her cool unworldliness. In addition, there is a full moon. He walks out into a gallery hung with pictures. The pictures add to his pensive mood.

> But by dim lights the portraits of the dead
> Have something ghastly, desolate and dread.
>
> (St. 17)

Among them are portraits of once lovely women:

And the pale smile of Beauties in the grave,
　　The charms of other days, in starlight gleams,
Glimmer on high; their buried locks still wave
　　Along the canvas; their eyes glance like dreams
On ours, or spars within some dusky cave,
　　But Death is imaged in their shadowy beams.
A picture is the past; even ere its frame
Be gilt, who sate hath ceased to be the same.

　　　　　　　　　　　　　　　　　　(St. 19)

Juan's state of mind, influenced by meditation on the pathos of
the death of beauty, makes his succumb to paralyzing fear when
"a monk, arrayed/ In cowl and beads, and dusky garb" (St. 21)
silently walks by him three times.

In the morning he still shows the effects of the fright he has
had. He is pensive, distraught, and pale. Both Adeline and
Aurora notice the change in him. Lord Henry remarks that he
looks as if he had seen the ghost of the Black Friar. Adeline then
takes her harp and sings a ballad of her own composition on the
Black Friar (the Black Friars are the Dominicans, an order
founded by St. Dominic, a thirteenth-century Italian) who
haunts the house of the Amundevilles. Why she does this, Byron
pretends he does not know:

Perhaps she merely had the simple project
　　To laugh him out of his supposed dismay;
Perhaps she might wish to confirm him in it,
　　Though why I cannot say—at least this minute.

　　　　　　　　　　　　　　　　　　(St. 51)

The effect of the song is to bring back Juan somewhat to his
former self.

In Stanza 55 the narrative turns away from the ghost of the
Black Friar to the business of a typical day at Lord Henry's,
which forms the second section of the canto. There is a race be-
tween greyhounds and a young race horse for the guests to watch.
A picture dealer comes to Lord Henry to get his opinion on a
Titian, for Lord Henry is a connoisseur and the friend of artists,

if not of art. An architect comes with plans for the restoration of Norman Abbey; two lawyers come on Lord Henry's business; two poachers caught in a steel trap have to be taken care of; and a young unmarried pregnant country girl must be cross-examined, for Lord Henry is a justice, and justices of the peace, says Byron, must

> . . . keep the game
> And morals of the country from caprices
> Of those who have not a license for the same.
>
> (St. 63)

The third section of the canto describes one of Lord Henry's public days, which he has either once a week or twice a month, to keep his political fences mended. The public day is an open house for the local squirearchy, who may drop in without a formal invitation. There is a great banquet for them at Lord Henry's. There is

> Great plenty, much formality, small cheer,—
> And everybody out of their own sphere.
>
> (St. 78)

At the banquet Juan is again confused and distracted, and his blunders "cost his host three votes." Moreover, he notices that Aurora is looking at him.

> And something like a smile upon her cheek. . . .
> Indicative of some surprise and pity.
>
> (Sts. 92-93)

In the meantime Adeline is busy "playing her grand role" and Juan

> . . . began to feel
> Some doubt how much of Adeline was *real;* . . .

> So well she acted all and every part
> By turns. . . .
>
> (Sts. 96-97)

After the last of the local guests have gone, Lady Adeline and her friends entertain themselves by making fun of those who have departed. Aurora and Juan do not take part in the game, Juan because he is still in a state of reverie. His silence is interpreted by Aurora as motivated by charity, and raises him in her esteem. Aurora has, in fact, renewed

> In him some feelings he had lately lost,
> Or hardened. . . .
>
> The love of higher things and better days;
>   The unbounded hope, and heavenly ignorance
> Of what is called the World, and the World's ways.
>   (Sts. 107-08)

These feelings seem to be chiefly associated with young love untainted by the world.

The last section of the canto is the resolution of the ghost episode. The feelings aroused in Juan by Aurora and the thoughts associated with them keep Juan awake that night and apprehensive of his spectral guest. As he sits in his bed, the door opens, and the ghost of the Black Friar enters his room. His first emotion is fear, which is soon succeeded by anger. He advances toward the ghost, reaches out a hand, and touches warm flesh. The ghost throws back its cowl and reveals the face of the Duchess Fitz-Fulke.

Commentary

In the first section of Canto XV we have a new Juan, or at least a Juan behaving in a way we have not seen him behave before. Never before has he shown any signs of fear, either in storm or in war, when taken by surprise or even when robbed — indeed, in any situation created by man or by physical nature. But Juan had never encountered a ghost before. Furthermore, Don Juan is a Roman Catholic and a man like Byron, who had had a Protestant upbringing, would be likely to think of all Catholics as being superstitious because of their belief in a state of Purgatory, relics, miracles, and so on. Possibly Byron is influenced by the Don Juan of the legend here. In Tirso de Molina's play, *The Rogue of Seville*, which had put the legend in literary circulation, the ghost of Don Gonzalo, whom Don Juan had killed in the first act, appears to Don Juan and invites him to dine with him beside his tomb. When Don Gonzalo's ghost disappears, Don Juan, who had just exclaimed, "What! Me afraid?" is covered with sweat and admits that his very heart seems frozen. There was, moreover, the legend of a ghost of a black monk at Newstead Abbey. Thomas Moore, in his life of his friend, said that Byron claimed he had seen the ghost himself. In Canto XV and in Stanzas 3-7 of Canto XVI, Byron seriously tried to persuade the reader that there might be such creatures as ghosts. Skeptical as Byron was, there was a vein of genuine religious belief in him.

The ghost section that concludes Canto XVI is entertaining, but we are apt to feel that Byron has merely tricked us, that he is working in a ghost to no great purpose because there was a ghost legend connected with Newstead Abbey and therefore with Norman Abbey. What did her frolic Grace Fitz-Fulke expect to gain by masquerading as a ghost that she would not have gained otherwise—in her own seductive person? If she had decided on a conquest of Don Juan, there was little to be gained by frightening him, as she had, and then entering his room. She had reason to believe that she had more to gain by simply dropping in on him, since she was charming and he no woman-hater. Why indulge in a foolish prank that might have frightened other Amundeville guests if they happened to meet her in her masquerade and might have resulted in injury or humiliation to herself? Byron has not motivated her act sufficiently, but he might have supplied the motivation in Canto XVII, had he lived to finish it.

Canto XVI, which Byron wrote between March 29 and May 6, 1823, almost a full year before his death on April 19, 1824, shows no diminution in imaginative power. It is as good in its own way as any other canto in *Don Juan*. There are relatively few non-narrative and non-descriptive stanzas in it. The ghost episode is not without interest; the account of Lord Henry's business day in the country is concise, pointed, and witty. The assembly of country guests shows nicely the landed politician at work feeding and flattering those who can be useful to him in the way of furnishing votes. The concluding line of the canto shows that Byron knew the value of and could create climax. The construction is good. The canto begins with the first part of the ghost episode and ends with its conclusion. Between the two parts, Byron carries out his satiric purpose by showing Lord Henry in different roles.

In the English cantos, which amount to more than a third of *Don Juan,* his narrative is rather thin, but Byron has created some of the most interesting people in *Don Juan,* and through and around them he held up the mirror to English aristocratic life in the early nineteenth century. The reflection is obviously a distorted one, but nevertheless it is factual as far as it goes, for Byron knew this society well at firsthand. He shows its members engaged in intrigue among themselves, maintaining a polite front while ceaselessly trying to win selfish advantages for themselves. Its women have no serious aim in life and its men are dull, pretentious, and unhappily married. They are all bored and spend their time in social activities of various kinds in the town or in the country. They are all other than what they seem to be.

CANTO XVII
(Unfinished)

Summary

There are three kinds of orphans: (1) the children who have lost their parents; (2) the children who receive no love from their parents; and (3) children who have no brothers or sisters. Of the three the most unfortunate are those who have lost their parents and are wealthy.

People should be tolerant of free discussion of all things, and the author, for one, will be among these.

Whether Juan gave in to the Duchess Fitz-Fulke the night before, or resisted her charms, the author refuses to say. When Juan comes to breakfast he looks wan and worn. The duchess "had a sort of air rebuked—/ Seemed pale and shivered" (St. 14). She looked as if she had not slept.

Commentary

The fourteen stanzas of Canto XVII introduce the question of possible moral development in Juan. He had developed in all other respects. Is he still amoral in matters of love? What went on between Juan and the ghostly Lady Fitz-Fulke? Did virtue or vice prevail in the case of Juan? Stanza 12 makes it clear that a conflict had taken place in Juan's soul. On the morning after, both Juan and the duchess looked tired, as if neither had slept. If virtue did not prevail in Juan's conscience, why should Byron say that the duchess had "a sort of air rebuked"?

Juan yielded to Donna Julia; he yielded to Haidée; he refused Gulbeyaz because she had used the wrong approach, but he was on the point of yielding when the coming of the sultan was announced; and he yielded to Catherine—and in each case the woman had been, so to speak, the aggressor. Has he yielded to the Duchess Fitz-Fulke or has he shown her the error of her wayward ways? If he has yielded, why should the duchess have "a sort of air rebuked"? Moreover, Aurora, by what she is, has shown Juan an ideal of purity and virtue that has not left him unmoved. She stands between him, as it were, and Fitz-Fulke duchesses. The question is a pertinent one but not easily solvable. Byron supplies us with only the single word *rebuked* to help us arrive at an answer. If it could be shown that Juan had said "no" to the duchess, it would mean that Byron was moving Juan toward an ideal of purity (and sexual immorality is practically the only moral weakness of Don Juan) represented in the flesh by Leila ("For like a day-dawn she was young and pure"— Canto XII, St. 61) and by Aurora, whose name means "daydawn." Unfortunately, the language of the three last stanzas of *Don Juan* can be interpreted in two different ways, and when the poem comes to an end the reader is left with a problem that he must solve for himself.

NOTES ON THE MAIN CHARACTERS

DON JUAN

At the age of sixteen Don Juan has completed his formal education and is ready to set out on the "grand tour" which, in England, often followed graduation from the university. Byron himself had made a grand tour in the Near East after he received his degree from Cambridge. Juan was the product of an experiment in education which was arranged for him by his mother. He had received instruction from tutors only and had not attended schools. He was taught the classics from expurgated editions and as a consequence had to learn the basic facts of life from experience. He had not been taught "natural history." His education had not prepared him for Donna Julias and Haidées. Since he belonged to the nobility, he was given instruction in the arts of war: riding, fencing, gunnery, and the techniques to be used in assaulting a fortress. His education also included an abundance of religious and moral instruction.

Juan is by nature kind, friendly, impulsive, courteous, courageous, and sensuous. He has all the virtues a boy of sixteen can reasonably be expected to have—except self-control in matters of sex. Sex education had not been a part of his formal instruction. His mother's system was therefore indirectly responsible for his fall from grace in Canto I.

By the time he is twenty-one, in Canto XVI, Juan has lost some of his impulsiveness and naivete. Experience had been his teacher after he left his home at sixteen or seventeen. He still has all his good qualities, but he has acquired a knowledge of the ways of the world and is able to analyze and judge that world. He is no longer at the mercy of impulse. Heart and head now work together.

DONNA JULIA

Donna Julia is a young woman of twenty-three who is married to a man of fifty. The personality of her husband is neither attractive nor repulsive; it is neutral. He is incapable of giving his wife the affection and comradeship that she needs. These she finds in Don Juan and therefore is powerfully attracted to him. She is not basically hypocritical but she is desperately in need of love. She does not know herself well, and when she begins to find in Don Juan what is lacking in her life, nature takes over and cooperates with her frustrations. She falls in love with Juan as she had not been able to fall in love with her husband. Her eyes are gradually opened to what is happening in her, but by this time love is so firmly rooted in her that she becomes a hypocrite both in regard to herself and in regard to her husband. She knows she should avoid Juan and she tries to resolve the conflict in herself by rationalizing. She tries to persuade herself that her love is only friendship. Her conscience becomes warped in the process. Once she falls, her conscience ceases to bother her, and it is Donna Julia the hardened sinner who tries to turn the tables on her husband in her brilliant invective when he bursts into her room in search of her lover.

HAIDÉE

Haidée is an ardent, beautiful and sensuous young woman in search of perfect love. She is all heart, and her mind has received little, if any, formal training. She has had religious instruction, however; Byron tells us that she is pious and has been taught the tenets of the Greek Orthodox Church. She is also not without experience in courtship. By the time she is seventeen she has had a number of marriage offers. She has turned down her suitors because none of them is exactly what she is looking for. Haidée is not entirely nature's child, as Byron once says she is. She has had some formal instruction in religion and she has had experience in the arts of courtship. She knows the difference between right and wrong, but her ardent nature is her enemy in moments of crisis. The pull of the flesh is strong in her. When she finds Juan lying unconscious on the shore of her island, she

> . . . deemed herself in common pity bound,
> As far as in her lay, "to take him in,
> A stranger" dying—with so white a skin.
>
> (Canto II, St. 129)

She possesses some of the courage and stubbornness of her father, as she shows when her father commands Juan to surrender.

LAMBRO

Lambro has become rich by smuggling, piracy, and slave trading. He has become hardened by the kind of life he had chosen to live. The only soft spot in his heart is his love for his motherless daughter and his love for his enslaved homeland. He is a man of inflexible will and rigid self-control. Externally he is calm and has the manners of a gentleman. There is a contradiction between what he is in appearance and what he is within—greedy, cruel, merciless, and passionate:

> Not that he was not sometimes rash or so,
>   But never in his real and serious mood;
> Then calm, concentrated, and still, and slow,
>   He lay coiled like the Boa in the wood;
> With him it never was a word and blow,
>   His angry word once o'er, he shed no blood,
> But in his silence there was much to rue,
> And his *one* blow left little work for *two.*
>
> (Canto III, St. 48)

JOHN JOHNSON

John Johnson is a practical man of the world who, like George Bernard Shaw's Bluntschli in *Arms and the Man,* has neither ideals nor illusions and who makes his living as a mercenary soldier. He believes that it is better to run away or surrender than to fight to the death. He is no martyr nor is he a coward. He will fight as long as he has a chance of winning. If he runs away or surrenders, he will return to fight again when the opportunity offers.

He takes life as it comes and believes in making the most of the present moment. When Juan suggests that he and Johnson overpower Baba and make their escape, Johnson recommends that they eat first and then weigh their chances of escaping. When Baba tries to persuade Johnson and Juan to be circumcised and become Moslems, Johnson replies that he will consider the proposition on a full stomach. His philosophy is a combination of common sense, stoicism, and opportunism.

GULBEYAZ

Like Donna Julia, the Sultana Gulbeyaz is a frustrated wife. She has to share her husband with three other wives and fifteen hundred concubines. Moreover, she is twenty-six and he is fifty-nine. Like Donna Julia she wants love and cannot get it. She has little self-control and is a creature of whims. When she sees the handsome Juan on his way to the slave market, she recklessly decides to buy him, even though by doing so she runs the risk of losing her own life. She lives in a culture in which life is cheap and is bought and sold. The punishment for infidelity is a quick death. That fact does not deter her. As the favorite wife of the sultan, she is accustomed to getting her way. When crossed or displeased her instinct is to punish and punish harshly. When she learns that Juan, as "Juanna," has shared the bed of the concubine Dudù, she resolves to destroy both of them, even though by doing so she is eliminating the one who might give her the love she so passionately desires.

SUWARROW

Suwarrow is a professional soldier and a man of limited outlook. He is completely devoted to his chosen occupation and does whatever is necessary to win battles. He has no false pride and no false notions of what is becoming to an officer. He is not a spit-and-polish general. He believes in putting first things first. If his men need training in the use of the bayonet, he will shed his general's jacket and train them himself. He is efficient and sees immediately what needs to be done. He is concerned with making his men good soldiers, not with their lives. He is not interested in saving lives but in winning victories. He spares neither himself, nor his men, nor the enemy. He is a generals' general, brave, brilliant, and successful. He respects military courage in others and is not immune to appeals to his rather limited supply of mercy and justice.

CATHERINE THE GREAT

In *Don Juan* the reader sees only a few aspects of the complex woman who was Catherine the Great. He sees her chiefly as sensualist and as an absolute sovereign who is extravagantly generous to her lovers. He does not see her as the woman who did much to Westernize Russia and who was keenly interested in raising the level of culture in Russia. Nor does he see her as the shrewd and unscrupulous diplomat that she was, nor as the czarina who added thousands of square miles to Russian territory. He does not see her as a foreign woman of obscure family who came to Russia as a czar's wife and who by dint of her talents became one of the greatest sovereigns in the history of Russia.

LORD HENRY AMUNDEVILLE

Lord Henry is a politician and man of the world. He courts the good opinion and the friendship of those who can help him. He is a member of the Privy Council and as such a capable and faithful servant of his country; at the same time he manages to serve his own interests. He combines patriotism and self-interest in such a way as to make the two identical. He is cautious, reserved, and proud. He is slow to judge men but once he has made up his mind about them, nothing will make him change it.

He likes the feeling of superiority, and for this reason deliberately seeks out the acquaintance of people he can feel superior to.

He is a somewhat cold-blooded individual and is unable to give his wife the kind of love she would like to have. He is not much older than she is; there is no disparity of age between them. What keeps their union from being an ideal one is a matter of temperament. At heart he is more interested in matters of business than he is in people. He is, however, proud of his beautiful and charming wife.

LADY ADELINE AMUNDEVILLE

On the surface Lady Adeline seems to be a somewhat frigid young woman, but at heart she is deeply passionate. This frustration of her strong feelings is a source of potential danger for her marriage. She loves her husband but her love for him costs her an effort.

She is thoroughly at home in her high social circle. She is, nevertheless, "no deep judge of character." Her beauty and her charming manners win the admiration of all. Her reputation is secure. She is the ideal politician's wife. She knows all the arts of pleasing those whose votes her husband needs. She moves among his constituents with an ease that astonishes a foreigner like Juan. Her courtesy and tact when she is among them is, however, only a mask. As soon as she is out of their company she joins with her friends in making fun of them.

She is drawn to Juan because she finds in him a warmth that is lacking in her husband. Like many women she is a matchmaker, at least in Juan's case. She wants him to marry one of a number of good "catches" whom she lists. Such a marriage would be a loveless one, and that fact quite possibly would assure room for herself in Juan's heart.

AURORA RABY

Young, beautiful, and noble, Aurora Raby is an outsider in the aristocratic society to which she belongs by birth. She is a Roman Catholic in a social class that is overwhelmingly Protestant. Unlike Juan, who is also a Roman Catholic, she is a believer who practices her faith. Don Juan's Roman Catholic faith seems to be limited to a willingness to kiss the pope's foot, and his morals are flexible in spite of the fact that he has been educated mainly by clergymen. Aurora's faith and morals are firmly grounded. She is innocent and, in contrast to Lady Adeline, she is charitable. She is sincere, austere "As far as her own gentle heart allowed" (Canto XV, St. 46), unworldly, and free from envy.

REVIEW QUESTIONS AND THEME TOPICS

1. *Don Juan* has sometimes been called an epic. Look up some definitions of epic and decide whether *Don Juan* may properly be called an epic or not.

2. Read Tirso de Molina's play *The Rogue of Seville* and write an essay comparing and contrasting de Molina's play and Byron's poem about Don Juan.

3. What is the controlling idea of Byron's *Don Juan?*

4. Look up some definitions of picaresque novel and write an essay on *Don Juan* as picaresque novel.

5. Judging from *Don Juan*, what are Byron's views on man? Provide evidence.

6. Determine the kind and amount of realism in *Don Juan*.

7. Judging from what he says about himself in *Don Juan*, what is Byron's philosophy of life?

8. Read the chapters on the history of the realistic novel in a standard history of the novel and decide whether or not Don Juan can be considered a realistic novel in verse.

9. Is Don Juan an interesting main character for a narrative poem? Supply evidence in support of your opinion.

10. Is it true that Don Juan is merely a character to whom things happen?

11. Discuss Byron's use of digression in *Don Juan*. Is it a welcome addition to his narrative or does it weaken Don Juan as a poem? Compare Henry Fielding's use of digression in *Tom Jones* with Byron's use of digression in *Don Juan*.

12. Keeping in mind the total narrative content of *Don Juan*, sketch a suitable conclusion for the poem that will be consistent with the character of Don Juan.

13. Write an essay on the male characters in *Don Juan*. Decide which of them is the most interesting and give the reasons why.

14. Write an essay on the female characters in *Don Juan*. Decide which of them is the most interesting and give the reasons why.

15. In your opinion, is Byron more successful in creating female characters than he is in creating male characters? Supply evidence.

16. Read Henry Fielding's *Tom Jones* and compare it as narrative with Byron's *Don Juan*.

17. Would Byron's *Don Juan* be more interesting and entertaining if written in prose?

18. Read three other treatments of the Don Juan legend, including the one in George Bernard Shaw's *Man and Superman*, and compare them with Byron's *Don Juan*.

19. What is the best episode in *Don Juan* from every point of view? Supply evidence to support your opinion.

20. What image of Byron as an individual emerges from a reading of *Don Juan?* Is this image consistent with that to be found in any good biography of Byron?

21. Compare and contrast Byron's *Don Juan* with his *Childe Harold's Pilgrimage.*

22. Discuss the part played by Donna Inez in the formation of Don Juan's character.

23. Read a reliable account of the life of Catherine the Great of Russia and decide whether Byron's characterization is historically accurate or not.

24. Read a reliable account of the life of Marshal Suvaroff (Suvorov) and decide whether Byron's characterization is historically accurate or not.

25. Compare and contrast Byron's Don Juan-Haidée episode with any earlier love story in verse.

26. What is the value of dialogue in narrative? How much dialogue does Byron use in *Don Juan?* Which canto contains the most dialogue? Compare that canto in literary quality with the others.

27. Make a list of the people satirized in *Don Juan.* For what faults does Byron satirize them?

28. Make a list of the subjects Byron makes digressive comments on in *Don Juan.*

29. Write a research paper on the long quarrel between Byron and Robert Southey.

30. Using *Don Juan* as your source of evidence, write an essay on Byron's theory of poetry.

SELECTED BIBLIOGRAPHY

Biography

MARCHAND, L. A. *Byron: A Biography.* 3 vols. New York: Knopf, 1957. The definitive biography.

Editions

COLERIDGE, E. H., and PROTHERO, R. E. (eds.). *The Works of Lord Byron.* 13 vols. London: John Murray, 1922.

MARCHAND, L. A. (ed.). *Don Juan.* Boston: Houghton Mifflin, 1958. (Paperback, Riverside Edition B40.) An inexpensive edition with good introduction and ample footnotes.

STEFFAN, T. G., and PRATT, W. W. (eds.). *Byron's Don Juan: A Variorum Edition.* 4 vols. Austin: University of Texas Press, 1957. The definitive edition of Byron's *Don Juan.*

Bibliography

SINGER, ARMAND. *A Bibliography of the Don Juan Theme.* Morgantown: University of West Virginia Press, 1954.

The Don Juan Theme

AUSTEN, JOHN. *The Story of Don Juan.* London: M. Secker, 1939.

MANDEL, OSCAR (ed.). *The Theatre of Don Juan: A Collection of Plays and Views.* Lincoln: University of Nebraska Press, 1963.

WEINSTEIN, LEO. *The Metamorphoses of Don Juan.* Stanford: Stanford University Press, 1959.

Criticism

BLOOM, HAROLD. *The Visionary Company: A Reading of English Romantic Poetry*. London: Faber & Faber, 1962.

BOSTETTER, EDWARD E. (ed.). *Twentieth Century Interpretations of Don Juan*. Englewood Cliffs, N.J.: Prentice-Hall, Inc., 1969.

BOWRA, C. M. *The Romantic Imagination*. Cambridge: Harvard University Press, 1949.

BOYD, ELIZABETH F. *Byron's Don Juan: A Critical Study*. New York: Humanities Press, 1958.

BROWNSTEIN, R. M. "Byron's *Don Juan:* Some Reasons for the Rhymes," *Modern Language Quarterly*, XXVIII (1967), 177-91.

CALVERT, W. J. *Byron: Romantic Paradox*. New York: Russell & Russell, 1962.

CHEW, S. C. *Byron in England: His Fame and Afterfame*. London: John Murray, 1924.

FUESS, CLAUDE M. *Lord Byron as a Satirist in Verse*. New York: Russell & Russell, 1964.

GARDNER, HELEN. *"Don Juan."* In PAUL WEST (ed.), *Byron: A Collection of Critical Essays*. N.J.: Prentice-Hall, 1963.

HORN, ANDRAS. *Byron's "Don Juan" and the Eighteenth-Century English Novel*. Bern: Francke Verlag, 1962.

JOHNSON, E. D. H. "Don Juan in England," *ELH*, XI (1944), 135-53.

KROEBER, KARL. *Romantic Narrative Art*. Madison: University of Wisconsin Press, 1960.

LAUBER, JOHN. *"Don Juan as Anti-Epic," Studies in English Literature,* VIII (1968), 607-19.

LOVELL, E. J., JR. *Byron, the Record of a Quest: Studies in a Poet's Concept of Nature.* Austin: University of Texas Press, 1949.

———. "Irony and Image in *Don Juan.*" In M. H. ABRAMS (ed.), *English Romantic Poets: Modern Essays in Criticism.* New York: Oxford University Press, 1960.

LUKE, H. J., JR. "The Publishing of Byron's *Don Juan,*" *PMLA,* LXXIX (1965), 199-209).

MARCHAND, L. A. *Byron's Poetry: A Critical Introduction.* Boston: Houghton Mifflin, 1965.

MARSHALL, W. H. *The Structure of Byron's Major Poems.* Philadelphia: University of Pennsylvania Press, 1962.

RIDENOUR, G. M. *The Style of "Don Juan."* New Haven: Yale University Press, 1960.

———. "The Mode of Byron's *Don Juan,*" *PMLA,* LXXIX (1964), 442-46.

RUTHERFORD, ANDREW. *Byron: A Critical Study.* Edinburgh: Oliver & Boyd, 1961.

STAVROU, C. N. "Religion in Byron's *Don Juan,*" *Studies in English Literature,* III (1963), 567-94.

STEFFAN T. G. "The Token-web, The Sea-Sodom, and Canto I of *Don Juan.*" In *University of Texas Studies in English.* Austin: University of Texas Press, 1947.

———. *Byron's Don Juan, I, The Making of a Masterpiece.* Austin: University of Texas Press, 1957. Best critical essay on *Don Juan.*

THOMPSON, JAMES R. "Byron's Plays and *Don Juan:* Genre and Myth," *Bucknell Review,* XV (1967), 22-38.

TRUEBLOOD, P. G. *The Flowering of Byron's Genius: Studies in Byron's Don Juan.* New York: Russell & Russell, 1962.

_____. *Lord Byron.* New York: Twayne Publishers, Inc., 1969. Excellent chapter on *Don Juan.*

VAN DOREN, MARK. *Mark Van Doren on Great Poems of Western Literature.* New York: Collier Books, 1962.

WILKIE, BRIAN. *Romantic Poets and Epic Tradition.* Madison: University of Wisconsin Press, 1965.

NOTES

NOTES

NOTES

NOTES

NOTES

NOTES

NOTES